Essential Portuguese Grammar

By

ALEXANDER da R. PRISTA

Formerly Instructor of Portuguese Language and Literature in New York University

DOVER PUBLICATIONS, INC.
NEW YORK

Essential Portuguese Grammar is a new work,
first published by Dover Publications, Inc., in 1966.

Library of Congress Catalog Card Number: 66-20416
International Standard Book Number
ISBN-13: 978-0-486-21650-8
ISBN-10: 0-486-21650-0

Manufactured in the United States by LSC Communications
21650032   2019
www.doverpublications.com

CONTENTS

CONTENTS

CONTENTS

INTRODUCTION

Essential Portuguese Grammar is based on the assumption that you plan to spend a limited number of hours studying Portuguese grammar and that your objective is simple everyday communication. This book is not a condensed outline of all aspects of Portuguese grammar. It is a series of hints to help you use more effectively and with greater versatility phrases and vocabulary that you have already learned.

How to Study Essential Portuguese Grammar

If you have already studied Portuguese in a conventional manner, you can use this book as a refresher by glancing through all of it first and then selecting those areas on which you wish to concentrate.

If you have never studied Portuguese grammar, then the following suggestions will be helpful:

1. Master several hundred useful phrases and expressions such as you will find in any good phrase book or in the *Listen & Learn Portuguese* course. You will understand the suggestions contained in *Essential Portuguese Grammar* more easily after you have achieved this basic working knowledge of Portuguese. The purpose of this book is to enable you to gain greater fluency once you have learned phrases and expressions, not to teach you to construct sentences from rules and vocabulary.

2. Read through *Essential Portuguese Grammar* at least once in its entirety. Don't be concerned if anything is not immediately clear to you. What may appear discouragingly difficult at first will become easier as your studies progress. But the first reading is necessary to acquaint you with terms and concepts peculiar to Portuguese grammar. Learning what these terms and concepts are will help you to improve your comprehension of Portuguese and to use more freely the expressions you already know. As you use Portuguese and hear it spoken, many of its grammatical patterns will become familiar to you. *Essential Portuguese Grammar* helps you to discover these patterns so that you can use them.

I

3. Go back to this book periodically. Sections which seem difficult or of doubtful benefit at first may prove extremely useful later.

4. For the most part, the book follows a logical order, taking up the major divisions of grammar in sequence. You will do best to follow this order. However, some students learn best when they study to answer an immediate question or need (e.g., how to form the comparative; how to conjugate the verb "to be," etc.). If you are one of these students, turn to the section that interests you. But read through the entire section, rather than just an isolated part. Individual remarks, taken out of context, are easily misunderstood.

5. Examples are given for every rule. It is helpful to memorize these examples. If you learn every example in *Essential Portuguese Grammar*, together with its literal translation, you will have encountered the basic difficulties of Portuguese and studied models for their solution.

6. You cannot study Portuguese systematically without an understanding of its grammar, and the use and understanding of grammatical terms is as essential as a knowledge of certain mechanical terms when you learn to drive a car. If your knowledge of grammatical terms is weak, read the Glossary of Grammatical Terms (p. 99) and refer to it whenever necessary.

In every language there are many ways to express the same thought. Some constructions are simple, others more difficult.

During your first experiments in communication, use a simple construction. Throughout *Essential Portuguese Grammar* you will find suggestions on how to avoid complicated constructions in favor of simpler ones. You may ultimately wish to master a more sophisticated way of expressing yourself. Be satisfied at first with the simplest.

As you begin to speak Portuguese, you will become aware of the areas in which you need the most help in grammar. If you have no one with whom to speak, speak mentally to yourself. In the course of a day see how many of the simple thoughts you've expressed in English you are able to turn into Portuguese. This kind of experimental self-testing will give direction to your study of grammar. Remember that you are studying this course in Portuguese not to pass an examination or to receive a certificate, but to communicate with others on a simple but useful level. *Essential Portu-*

guese Grammar is not the equivalent of a formal course of study at a university. Although it could serve as a supplement to such a course, its primary aim is to help the adult study on his own. Indeed, no self-study or academic course or series of courses is ever ideally suited to all students. You must rely on and be guided by your own rate of learning and your own requirements and interests. *Essential Portuguese Grammar* makes self-study easier.

If this or any other grammar tends to inhibit you in speaking Portuguese or in using what you have learned through phrase books, conversation courses, or the *Listen & Learn* records, curtail your study of grammar until you feel it will really assist rather than hinder your speaking. Your objective is speaking, and you *can* learn to speak a language without learning its grammar. But because of its systematic approach, grammar is a short-cut to language learning for those who feel at home with it. The fundamental purpose of *Essential Portuguese Grammar* is to help you by eliminating hit-or-miss memorization.

SUGGESTIONS FOR VOCABULARY BUILDING

1. Study words and word lists that answer real and preferably immediate personal needs. If you are planning to travel in the near future, your motivation and orientation are clear cut and *Listen & Learn Portuguese* or a good travel phrase book will provide you with the material you need. But select from this material that specifically applies to your case. For instance, if you don't plan to motor, don't spend time studying the parts of the car. If you like foreign foods, study the supplementary Portuguese food list in *Listen & Learn Portuguese*. Even if you do not plan to travel in the near future, you will probably learn more quickly by imagining a travel situation.

2. Memorize by association. Phrase books and *Listen & Learn Portuguese* usually give associated word lists. If you use a dictionary, don't memorize words haphazardly but choose words which are related and belong to the same family.

3. Study the specialized vocabulary of your profession, business, or hobby. If you are interested in real estate, learn the terms associated with property, buying, selling, leasing, etc. If you are interested in mathematics, acquire a vocabulary in this science. Many of these specialized words can be used in other areas too. You may not find specialized vocabularies in ordinary phrase books, but a good dictionary will help you to make up a list for your own use.

Similarities between English and Portuguese Vocabulary

It will help you to expand your Portuguese vocabulary if you remember that many Portuguese words are similar in appearance and meaning to English words. Notice: *o perfume* (the perfume), *o telefone* (the telephone), *a rosa* (the rose), *o momento* (the moment), *comercial* (commercial).

Here are some common differences in spelling between English and Portuguese:

English *k* or *ck* = Port. *c* (before *a*, *o*
        or *u*)   sa*ck*—sa*c*o
      qu (before *e* or par*k*—par*qu*e; che*ck*—
        (*i*)   che*qu*e
 „ *ph*   „ *f*   *ph*rase—*f*rase;
            *ph*iloso*ph*y—*f*iloso*f*ia
 „ *th*   „ *t*   *th*eater—*t*eatro
 „ *tion* „ *ção*   na*tion*—na*ção*
 „ *ty*   „ *dade* nationali*ty*—nacionali*dade*
 „ *ism* „ *ismo* national*ism*—nacional*ismo*
 „ *ist*   „ *ista*   national*ist*—nacional*ista*
 „ *ize*   „ *izar*   national*ize*—nacional*izar*
 „ *ous* „ *oso*   fam*ous*—fam*oso*

Study this list of words, observing the differences between English and Portuguese. Note that *rr* and *ss* (and rarely *mm* and *nn*) are the only double consonants used in Portuguese:

ENGLISH	PORTUGUESE
area	área
aroma	aroma
hotel	hotel
perfume	perfume
professor	professor
radio	rádio
annual	anual
commercial	comercial
idea	idéia
special	especial
telephone	telefone

ENGLISH	PORTUGUESE
arithmetic	aritmética
list	lista
mass	massa
moment	momento
monarch	monarca
problem	problema
rheumatism	reumatismo
cause	causa
curve	curva
figure	figura
medicine	medicina
rose	rosa
applause	aplauso
minister	ministro
minute	minuto
territory	território
tube	tubo
use	uso
delicious	delicioso
generous	generoso
studious	estudioso
geography	geografia
history	história
action	acção*
collection	colecção*
expression	expressão

* The c in these words is silent and is generally omitted in Brazilian spelling: ação, coleção. The same is true of the p in words like adoptar (to adopt), spelled adotar in Brazil.

WORD ORDER

Word order in Portuguese is frequently the same as in English. This, added to the similarities between many English and Portuguese words, often makes it easy to understand a Portuguese sentence even with a minimum knowledge of grammar. Compare the following sentences in Portuguese and in English:

Lisboa é a capital de Portugal.
Lisbon is the capital of Portugal.

Os turistas geralmente visitam os pontos de interesse.
The tourists generally visit the points of interest.

HOW TO FORM QUESTIONS

You can turn a simple statement into a question in one of the following three ways:

1. Leave the sentence as it is and simply add a question mark at the end. When speaking, raise your voice at the end of the sentence. This is often done in English too.

Seu pai fala inglês?
Your father speaks English?

Ela é americana?
She is American?

2. Invert the normal order and place the verb before the subject.

Fala seu pai inglês?
[Speaks your father English?]
Does* your father speak English?

É ela americana?
Is she American?

3. Leave the sentence as it is and simply add one of the following phrases at the end: *não?* [no?]; *não é?* [not is?]; *não é verdade?* [not is truth?]; *não é assim?* [not is so?]. These phrases are the Portuguese equivalents of such English phrases as "isn't it?" "don't you?" "aren't you?" etc.

Sua mãe fala francês, *não é verdade?*
Your mother speaks French, *doesn't she?*

Ele† estava lá, *não é assim?*
He was there, *wasn't he?*

---

* The verb "to do"—used in English questions such as "*Do* you want some coffee?"—is not used this way in Portuguese.

† The words *ele* (he), *eles* (they), *este* (this), *estes* (these), *esse* (that), *esses* (those), *aquele* (that) and *aqueles* (those) were once spelled with a circumflex accent on their first *e*, and appear with the accent in Dover's *Listen & Learn Portuguese*. This accent, abolished in such cases by the latest orthographic agreement between Portugal and Brazil, will not be used in the present book, although particularly in Brazil it continues to be used.

9

Interrogative Words

Most questions, in Portuguese as in English, begin with a question word such as "when?" "where?" "how?" Study the following list carefully:

Como?	How?	*Como* se diz em português? [How itself (it) says in Portuguese?] *How* do you say (this) in Portuguese?
Quando?	When?	*Quando* parte para o Brasil? *When* are you leaving for Brazil?
Onde?	Where?	*Onde* está o livro? *Where* is the book?
*Porque?**	Why?	*Porque* estuda português? *Why* do you study Portuguese?
Quem?	Who?	*Quem* são eles? *Who* are they?
De quem?	Whose?	*De quem* é esta casa? [Of whom is this house?] *Whose* house is this?
Que?	What? Which?†	*Que* diz meu irmão? *What* does my brother say? *Que* rua é esta? *What* street is this? *Que* professor disse isso? *Which* teacher said that?

* When it stands alone, *porque* is written with a circumflex:
Estuda português. *Porquê?*
You study Portuguese. *Why?*
† *See footnote on next page.*

Qual?	Which?	Which	*Qual* deles é o capitão?
(PL. *Quais?*)	one(s)?†		*Which* (*one*) of them is the captain?

Quais são os livros de Manuel?
[*Which* are the books of Manuel?]
Which (*ones*) are Manuel's books?

Quanto?	How much?	*Quanto* custa isto? *How much* does this cost?

Quantos?	How many?	*Quantos* dias há numa semana? *How many* days are there in a week?
(FEM. *Quantas?*)		

Quantas semanas há num ano?
How many weeks are there in a year?

† Notice that, in translating "which," *que* is used as the adjective (immediately followed by a noun: "which teacher") and *qual* as the pronoun ("which (one)": always implying a choice among a group of persons or things).

O que is often used instead of *que* to translate the interrogative pronoun "what":
O que diz meu irmão?
What does my brother say?

When *que* (or *o que*) stands alone, a circumflex is added to the *e*:
Deseja alguma coisa. *O quê?*
You want something. *What?*

NOUNS AND ARTICLES

Gender of Portuguese Nouns

All Portuguese nouns are either masculine or feminine. In general, nouns denoting male persons or animals are masculine, and nouns denoting female persons or animals are feminine. This rule, however, is of no help in identifying the gender of the countless nouns which do not denote persons or animals. On page 15 we give some hints on the identification of gender, but the best way is to memorize the definite article together with the noun.

The Definite Article

In Portuguese, the definite article agrees in gender and number with the noun it accompanies. English is simpler in this respect, for the same form, "the," is used for all nouns, singular or plural. The forms of the definite article in Portuguese are:

MASC. SING.: *o*   MASC. PL.: *os*
FEM. SING.: *a*   FEM. PL.: *as*

Examples of the articles together with nouns:

	SING.	PL.
MASC.	*o* irmão, the brother	*os* irmãos, the brothers
FEM.	*a* irmã, the sister	*as* irmãs, the sisters

Plurals of Nouns

1. The majority of Portuguese nouns end in a vowel and simply add an *s* to form the plural:

a casa (the house)   as casa*s* (the houses)
o livro (the book)   os livro*s* (the books)
a lei (the law)   as lei*s* (the laws)

2. Nouns ending in -*r* or -*z* add -*es* to form the plural:

a mulher (the woman)   as mulher*es* (the women)
o rapaz (the boy)   os rapaz*es* (the boys)

3. Nouns ending in -s form their plural in one of two ways:

(a) If the last syllable is stressed, -es is added to the singular form:

 o país (the country) os países (the countries)

(b) If the last syllable is not stressed, the noun remains unchanged in the plural:

 o lápis (the pencil) os lápis (the pencils)

4. Nouns ending in -m change the -m to -ns in the plural:

o homem (the man) os homens (the men)
o jardim (the garden) os jardins (the gardens)
a viagem (the journey) as viagens (the journeys)

5. Nouns ending in -al, -el, -ol and -ul change their -l to -is:

o animal (the animal) os animais (the animals)
o papel (the paper) os papéis (the papers)
o sol (the sun) os sóis (the suns)
o paul (the swamp) os pauis (the swamps)

6. Nouns ending in -il form their plural in one of two ways, depending on whether the -il is stressed or unstressed:

(a) Stressed -il is changed to -is:

 o barril (the barrel) os barris (the barrels)

(b) Unstressed -il is changed to -eis:

 o fóssil (the fossil) os fósseis (the fossils)

7. Nouns ending in -ão generally form their plural in one of the following ways:

(a) -ão changes to -ões:

 a lição (the lesson) as lições (the lessons)

(b) -ão changes to -ãos:

 o irmão (the brother) os irmãos (the brothers)

(c) -ão changes to -ães:

 o cão (the dog) os cães (the dogs) *

* Those familiar with Spanish may find it easier to remember the various plural endings of Portuguese ão-nouns by comparing them with the equivalent endings in Spanish:

	SPANISH	PORTUGUESE
SING.	-ón (lección)	-ão (lição)
	-ano (hermano)	-ão (irmão)
	-án (capitán)	-ão (capitão)
PL.	-ones (lecciones)	-ões (lições)
	-anos (hermanos)	-ãos (irmãos)
	-anes (capitanes)	-ães (capitães)

By far the greatest number of nouns ending in -*ão* form their plural by changing -*ão* to -*ões*. Therefore, when in doubt, change -*ão* to -*ões* and you will be understood.

Nouns that change -*ão* to -*ães* are very few. The following sentence will help you to remember those most frequently used:

SING.   O capit*ão* alem*ão* dá p*ão* ao c*ão*.*
         The German captain gives bread to the dog.

PL.   Os capit*ães* alem*ães* d*ão* p*ães* aos c*ães*.
       The German captains give loaves of bread to the dogs.

SUMMARY TABLE OF NOUN PLURALS

	SING.	PL.
noun ends in vowel:	a casa	as casas
noun ends in -*r* or -*z*:	o rapaz	os rapazes
noun ends in -*s*:		
(a) last syllable stressed:	o país	os países
(b) last syllable unstressed:	o lápis	os lápis
noun ends in -*m*:	o homem	os homens
noun ends in -*al*, -*el*, -*ol*, -*ul*:	o animal	os animais
noun ends in -*il*:		
(a) last syllable stressed:	o barril	os barris
(b) last syllable unstressed:	o fóssil	os fósseis
noun ends in -*ão*:	a lição	as lições
	o irmão	os irmãos
	o cão	os cães

Noun Suffixes

A special feature of Portuguese nouns is that their meaning can be modified by the addition of suffixes. Thus *homem* (man) can become *homenzinho* (small man) or *homenzarrão* (huge man). *Mulher*

* In this mnemonic sentence, *alemão* (German) is, strictly speaking, an adjective, but the noun *o alemão* (the German) forms its plural in exactly the same way.

(woman) can become *mulherinha* (small woman), *mulherona* (big, strong woman) or *mulherão* (big, masculine woman).   The use of these and other suffixes to express various shades of meaning is very frequent in idiomatic Portuguese and it is well for you to be aware of it, even if you do not make use of suffixes yourself.

Hints on the Identification of Gender

We have already said that the best way for you to remember the gender of a noun is to memorize the noun together with its article. There are, however, a few general rules which can help you in recognizing and remembering the gender of a noun.

1. You can recognize the gender of a noun by its ending.

(a) Nouns ending in -*o*,* -*im*, -*om* and -*um* are generally masculine: *o médico* (the doctor), *o fim* (the end), *o som* (the sound), *o atum* (the tuna).

(b) Nouns ending in -*a*, -*ção*, -*dade* and -*gem* are generally feminine: *a criada* (the maid), *a acção* (the action), *a caridade* (the charity), *a bagagem* (the baggage).

Exceptions: *o dia* (the day), *o poeta* (the poet), *o mapa* (the map), *o telegrama* (the telegram) and a number of others.

2. The gender of a noun may be recognized by its meaning.

MASC. (a) The names of male persons and animals are almost always masculine: *o pai* (the father), *o leão* (the lion).

(b) The names of the months are masculine: *o Abril* (April).

(c) The names of oceans, rivers, lakes and mountains are masculine: *o Atlântico*, (the Atlantic), *o Amazonas* (the Amazon), *o lago Erie* (Lake Erie), *os Alpes* (the Alps).

FEM. (d) The names of female persons and animals are usually feminine: *a mãe* (the mother), *a leoa* (the lioness).

Masculine and Feminine Forms of the Same Noun

You may find it useful to recognize the following changes in nouns:

(1) Changing the final vowel can make a masculine noun feminine:

---

* Not to be confused with the ending -*ão*, which is no sure indication of gender. (The ending -*ção*, however, makes a noun feminine.)

Francisco (Francis)—Francisca (Frances)
filho (son)—filha (daughter)

(2) Some feminine nouns are formed by adding -a to the masculine form:

cantor (singer, masc.)—cantora (singer, fem.)

(3) Dropping the final vowel and adding certain suffixes can make a masculine noun feminine:

poeta (poet)—poetisa (poetess)

(4) Some nouns refer to both male and female persons and adjust their gender accordingly:

o estudante (the student, masc.)—a estudante (the student, fem.)
o pianista (the pianist, masc.)—a pianista (the pianist, fem.)

Common Prepositions and the Definite Article

The most common Portuguese prepositions when used together with the definite article are contracted as follows:

PREPOSITION	DEFINITE ARTICLE			
	SINGULAR		PLURAL	
	o	a	os	as
a, to, at	ao	à	aos	às
de, of, from	do	da	dos	das
em, in, on	no	na	nos	nas
por, by, for	pelo	pela	pelos	pelas

Determine first what the proper form of the definite article is and then use the contracted form that corresponds to it.

Dei a minha bagagem ao motorista.
I gave my baggage to the driver.

Não sabemos o nome da rua.
We do not know the name of the street.

Deixou os papéis no automóvel.
He left the papers in the automobile.

Foi acompanhado pelas mulheres.
He was accompanied by the women.

The Indefinite Article

In English the indefinite article "a" becomes "an" when it precedes a vowel. In Portuguese the indefinite article agrees in gender with the noun it accompanies.
Study the following:

MASC. *um*   *um* quarto (a room); *um* avião (an airplane)
FEM. *uma*   *uma* janela (a window); *uma* actriz (an actress)

The indefinite article has no plural in English. Portuguese uses plural forms of *um* and *uma* (*uns* and *umas*, respectively) to express an indefinite plural ("some"): *uns* homens (some men), *umas* mulheres (some women).

The common prepositions *de* and *em* form contractions with the indefinite article as follows:

PREPOSITION	INDEFINITE ARTICLE			
	SINGULAR (= "a")		PLURAL (= "some")	
	um	*uma*	*uns*	*umas*
de, of, from	dum	duma	duns	dumas
em, in, on	num	numa	nuns	numas

Quem pode esquecer o perfume *duma* rosa?
Who can forget the fragrance *of a* rose?

Pôs a pílula *num* copo de água.
He put the pill *in a* glass of water.

ADJECTIVES

Agreement of Adjectives with Nouns

In Portuguese, adjectives agree in gender and number with the nouns they accompany. A masculine singular noun requires a masculine singular adjective, a feminine singular noun a feminine singular adjective, etc. In English, the use of adjectives is simpler because they are invariable: a *green* dress, two *green* dresses.

Feminine Singular Forms of Adjectives

Feminine singular adjectives are formed from the masculine singular in a variety of ways:

1. Most Portuguese adjectives end in -*o* in the masculine singular (*branco*, white; *alto*, high; *velho*, old). These adjectives change the -*o* to -*a* in the feminine singular:

MASC. SING.	FEM. SING.
o homem nov*o*	a mulher nov*a*
(the young man)	(the young woman)
o livro branc*o*	a casa branc*a*
(the white book)	(the white house)

2. Adjectives ending in -*e* in the masculine singular are generally unchanged in the feminine singular:

o vestido verd*e*	a bolsa verd*e*
(the green dress)	(the green purse)
um homem pobr*e* mas alegr*e*	uma mulher pobr*e* mas alegr*e*
(a poor but happy man)	(a poor but happy woman)

3. Masculine singular adjectives ending in a consonant generally remain unchanged in the feminine singular:

um homem amável	uma pessoa amável
(a pleasant man)	(a pleasant person)
o céu azul	a cadeira azul
(the blue sky)	(the blue chair)

18

o senso comum	uma flor comum
(common sense)	(a common flower)
o rapaz feliz	a mãe feliz
(the happy boy)	(the happy mother)

Exception: Many adjectives indicating nationality that end in *-ês* and *-l*, as well as some adjectives ending in *-or*, form the feminine by adding *-a* to the masculine form:

um rio inglês	a língua inglesa
(an English river)	(the English language)
o cavalo espanhol	a terra espanhola
(the Spanish horse)	(the Spanish land)
o homem encantador	a mulher encantadora
(the charming man)	(the charming woman)

4. Adjectives ending in *-ão* drop the final *-o* in the feminine:

o vinho alemão	a cerveja alemã
(the German wine)	(the German beer)

5. Adjectives ending in *-u* (not *-eu*!) add *-a* to form the feminine:

o arroz cru	a carne crua
(the uncooked rice)	(the raw meat)

6. Adjectives ending in *-eu* change *-eu* to *-eia*:

o clima europeu	a cooperação europeia
(the European climate)	(European cooperation)

7. Important irregular feminine singulars you should remember are the feminines of *bom* (good) and *mau* (bad), which are *boa* and *má*, respectively:

um bom filho	uma boa filha
(a good son)	(a good daughter)
o mau tempo	uma má estação
(the bad weather)	(a bad season)

8. The numeral adjective *dois* (two) has the feminine form *duas*.

Plurals of Adjectives

In general, Portuguese adjectives form their plural in the same manner as the nouns with the corresponding endings. (Note: This may not be the same ending as on the noun the adjective is accompanying!)

The cases shown in the following table are just like the noun plurals summarized in the table on page 14:

	SING.	PL.
adjective ends in vowel:	novo	novos
	espanhola	espanholas
adjective ends in -r or -z:	encantador	encantadores
	feliz	felizes
adjective ends in -m:	comum	comuns
adjective ends in -al, -el, -ol, -ul:	usual	usuais
	amável	amáveis
	espanhol	espanhóis
	azul	azuis
adjective ends in -il:		
(a) last syllable stressed:	civil	civis
(b) last syllable unstressed:	difícil	difíceis

Note the following case in which adjective plurals are different from noun plurals:

	SING.	PL.
adjective ends in -s:	inglês	ingleses

(just like adjectives ending in -r or -z)

Remember the following unusual or irregular adjective plurals:

SING.	PL.
alemão (German, MASC.)	alemães
alemã (German, FEM.)	alemãs
simples (simple)	simples

Position of Adjectives

In Portuguese the adjective usually follows the noun:

uma língua *difícil*, a *difficult* language
um rapaz *estudioso*, a studious boy

a maçã *madura*, the *ripe* apple
relações *comerciais*, *commercial* relations

A number of very common adjectives, however, often precede the noun in Portuguese, as in English:

bom, good	um *bom* automóvel (a *good* automobile)
belo, beautiful, handsome, fine	um *belo* presente (a *beautiful* gift)
mau, bad	um *mau* pai (a *bad* father)
grande, big, large, great	uma *grande* aldeia (a *large* village)
longo, long	uma *longa* ausência (a long absence)
breve, short	a *breve* carta (the *short* letter)
novo, new, young	os *novos* sapatos (the *new* shoes)
muito, much, many	*muita* dor (much pain); *muitos* anos (many years)*
primeiro, *segundo*, etc., first, second, etc.	a *primeira* vez (the *first* time)

Note: An adjective that normally follows a noun may take on a different connotation when placed before the noun, and vice versa. Compare:

um homem *grande*	a *large* man
um *grande* homem	a *great* man
o *bom* ano	the *good, prosperous* year
o ano *bom*	the *New* Year

* Do not confuse this variable adjective *muito, muita, muitos, muitas* (much, many) with the invariable adverb *muito* (very, a lot): Ele está *muito* cansado (He is very tired). Ela está *muito* cansada (She is *very* tired).

ADVERBS

In English, adverbs are often formed by adding -*ly* to the adjective: sure, sure*ly*; quiet, quiet*ly*. In Portuguese, adverbs are formed in a similar way, by adding -*mente* to the feminine singular of the adjective. Study this table:

ADJECTIVE		ADVERB
MASC. SING.	FEM. SING.	
claro (clear)	clara	clara*mente* (clearly)
sincero (sincere)	sincera	sincera*mente* (sincerely)
amável (pleasant)	amável	amàvel*mente* (pleasantly)
cortês (courteous)	cortês	cortês*mente* (courteously)
alegre (cheerful)	alegre	alegre*mente* (cheerfully)

Respondia sempre muito *cortêsmente*.
He always answered very *courteously*.

Estavam *sinceramente* felizes.
They were *sincerely* happy.

Observations on adverbial forms:

1. When two or more adverbs that normally end in -*mente* are used together, generally only the last one takes the ending, but all of them show the feminine singular form of the basic adjective:

Ele caminhava *vagarosa, resoluta* e *corajosamente*.
He walked *slowly, resolutely* and *courageously*.

2. The form of several common adverbs is identical with the masculine singular form of the adjective (without additional endings), although the -*mente* form also exists for some of them:

breve (or *brevemente*), shortly, soon
próximo (or *pròximamente*), nearly
raro (or *raramente*), rarely
certo (or *certamente*), certainly
barato, cheap(ly)

caro, dear(ly)
pronto (or *prontamente*), promptly, quickly

3. You should memorize the following list of other common adverbs that do not end in -*mente*:

bem	well	João canta muito *bem*.
		John sings very *well*.
mal	badly	Tudo saiu *mal*.
		Everything turned out *badly*.
demais	too, too much	Ele chegou tarde *demais*.*
		He arrived *too* late.
(um) pouco	(a) little	*Um pouco* mais, por favor.
		A little more, please.
tão, tanto	so, so much	Ele é *tão* (or *tanto*) pequeno.
		He is *so* small.
sempre	always	Porque é *sempre* triste?
		Why is he *always* sad?
logo	at once, immediately	O comboio partiu *logo*.
		The train left *immediately*.
aqui, cá	here	Este livro está *aqui*.
		This book is *here*.
aí	there (near the person addressed)	Esse livro está *aí*.
		That book is *there* [near you].
ali, acolá, lá	over there (away from the speaker and the person addressed)	Aquele livro está *acolá*.
		That book is *over there*.

* Note that *demais* always follows the word it modifies. In general, adverbs precede the word they modify but follow the verb; exceptions to this rule are mainly for the sake of emphasis or euphony.

COMPARISONS OF ADJECTIVES AND ADVERBS

Comparisons of Inequality

There are two ways of expressing comparison in English. You can add *-er* or *-est* to some adjectives and adverbs (soft, soft*er*, soft*est*; soon, soon*er*, soon*est*). Or you can place the words "more" or "less," "most" or "least" before these and other adjectives and adverbs (interesting, *more* or *less* interesting, *most* or *least* interesting; quickly, *more* or *less* quickly, *most* or *least* quickly).

In Portuguese there is only one way of expressing such comparisons of inequality. Place the words *mais* (more), *o mais* (most), or *menos* (less), *o menos* (least) before the adjective or adverb. In adjectives, the definite article in *o mais* and *o menos* must agree in gender and number with the accompanying noun.

Study the following table:

forte, strong	*mais* forte, stronger	*o mais* forte, (the) strongest
	menos forte, less strong	*o menos* forte, (the) least strong
interessante, interesting	*mais* interessante, more interesting	*o mais* interessante, (the) most interesting
	menos interessante, less interesting	*o menos* interessante, (the) least interesting
claramente, clearly	*mais* claramente, more clearly	*o mais* claramente, most clearly
	menos claramente, less clearly	*o menos* claramente, least clearly

João é forte, mas José é *mais* forte. Francisco é *o mais* forte.
John is strong, but Joseph is stronger. Francis is the strongest.

A minha viagem foi muito interessante. A viagem de Maria foi *menos* interessante. A viagem de Fernanda foi *a menos* interessante.

24

My trip was very interesting. Maria's trip was less interesting. Fernanda's trip was the least interesting.

Faça favor de falar *mais* claramente, *o mais* claramente possível.
Please speak more clearly, as clearly as possible.

Irregular Comparative Forms

While most adjectives and adverbs express comparison regularly, some very common adjectives and adverbs have irregular forms of comparison. In a few of these cases the regular forms are also used.

ADJ.	bom, good	*melhor*, better	o *melhor*, best
	mau, bad	*pior*, worse	o *pior*, worst
	grande, big, large	mais grande OR *maior*, larger, greater	o mais grande OR o *maior*, largest, greatest
	pequeno, small	mais pequeno OR *menor*, smaller	o mais pequeno OR o *menor*, smallest
ADV.	bem, well	*melhor*, better	o *melhor*, best
	mal, badly	*pior*, worse	o *pior*, worst
	muito, much, very	*mais*, more	o *mais*, most
	pouco, little	*menos*, less	o *menos*, least

Este é *o melhor* hotel da* nossa cidade.
This is *the best* hotel in our city.

Este lápis escreve *pior* que aquele.
This pencil writes *worse* than that one.

Qual é *o* livro *mais interessante* da sua colecção?
What is *the most interesting* book in your collection?

The Absolute Superlative

Portuguese frequently uses the adjective or adverb form that ends in *-íssimo*. This form is called the absolute superlative because it implies no comparison. A similar absolute judgment is expressed in English when you say *very smart* or *extremely smart*,† or when you

* Note that the word "in" when used after a superlative is translated by *de* in Portuguese.

† Of course, it is also possible to use *muito* (very) or *extremamente* (extremely) with the simple form of the adjective, as in English.
Ele é *riquíssimo*.   OR   Ele é *extremamente rico*.
He is *extremely rich*.

use *excellent* instead of *the best.* Compare the meaning of "This wine is excellent" with "This is the best wine I have ever tasted."

To form the absolute superlative:

1. When the basic adjective ends in an unstressed vowel, drop the vowel and add *-íssimo*: alt*o* (high), alt*íssimo* (very high); verd*e* (green), verd*íssimo* (extremely green).   Note the spelling changes in *-co* and *-go* adjectives: ri*co* (rich), ri*quíssimo* (very rich); lar*go* (wide), lar*guíssimo* (very wide).   Irregular: ami*go* (friendly), ami*císsimo* (very friendly).

2. When the adjective ends in *-s*, merely add *-íssimo*: português (Portuguese), portugues*íssimo* (very Portuguese).

3. Observe what happens with adjectives ending in *-ão*, *-vel* and *-z*: s*ão* (healthy), san*íssimo* (extremely healthy); am*ável* (pleasant), ama*bilíssimo* (very pleasant); fero*z* (fierce), fero*císsimo* (very fierce).

4. The absolute superlative forms of *fácil* (easy) and *difícil* (difficult) are *facílimo* and *dificílimo*.

5. For adverbs which end in *-mente*, the *-íssimo* is added to the adjective before *-mente*: alegre (cheerful), alegr*íssimo* (very cheerful), alegr*íssima*mente (very cheerfully); cortês (courteous), cortes*íssimo* (very courteous), cortes*íssima*mente (very courteously); possível (possible), possibil*íssimo* (extremely possible), possibil*íssima*mente (very possibly).   Remember that the form of the adjective to which *-mente* is added is the feminine singular: alegríssim*a*.

Lisboa é uma cidade *interessantíssima.*
Lisbon is a *very interesting* city.

Camões é um *grandíssimo* poeta.
Camões is a *very great* poet.

Este cão ladra *ferocíssimamente.*
This dog barks *very ferociously.*

The Word "Than"

The word *than* used in comparisons (I am taller *than* he is) is generally translated by *que* or *do que* in Portuguese:

Meu pai é mais rico *que* (OR *do que*) seu irmão.
My father is richer *than* his brother.

The form *do que* is always used when a clause follows the "than":

Estou menos feliz *do que* ele pensa.

I am less happy *than* he thinks.

But when the "than" is followed by a numeral or a word expressing quantity, the "than" is translated by *de*:

Isto custa mais *de* dez dólares.

This costs more *than* ten dollars.

Comparisons of Equality

The "as . . . as" of comparisons of equality (She is *as* pretty *as* her sister) is translated in Portuguese either by *tão . . . como* or by *tão . . . quanto*. As in English, the two words are placed around the adjective or adverb: *tão* simples *como* (*as* simple *as*), *tão* pronto *quanto* (*as* quickly *as*).

Sou *tão* rico *como* eles.

I am *as* rich *as* they.

O nosso hotel é *tão* cómodo *quanto* (OR *como*) o seu.

Our hotel is *as* comfortable *as* yours.

EXPRESSING POSSESSION

In English you can say either "the teacher's book" or "the book of the teacher." There is no form corresponding to the apostrophe s in Portuguese. A form comparable to "the book of the teacher" is used.

a esposa do general   o chapéu de minha mãe

the general's wife   my mother's hat

Possessive Adjectives

In Portuguese the possessive adjective is almost always preceded by the definite article. Study the two words together as a unit.

MASC. SING.	FEM. SING.	MASC. PL.	FEM. PL.	
o meu	a minha	os meus	as minhas	my, mine
o teu	a tua	os teus	as tuas	your, yours (fam. sing.)
o seu	a sua	os seus	as suas	his, her, hers, its; your, yours (polite)
o nosso	a nossa	os nossos	as nossas	our, ours
o vosso	a vossa	os vossos	as vossas	your, yours (formal fam. pl.)
o seu	a sua	os seus	as suas	their, theirs; your, yours (polite)

Observations on possessive adjectives:

1. Possessive adjectives agree in gender and number with the noun they accompany, that is, with the thing possessed:

Onde está *a nossa* bagagem?
Where is *our* baggage?

Senhor, eis *o seu* passaporte.
Sir, here is *your* passport.

28

Senhora, eis *o seu* passaporte.
Madam, here is *your* passport.

Estou visitando *os meus* amigos.
I am visiting *my* friends.

O seu impermeável e *as suas* luvas estão acolá.
Your raincoat and *your* gloves are over there.

2. The form *o seu* (*a sua, os seus, as suas*) may mean "his," "her," "its," "their," or "your (polite)," but in the normal course of a conversation there should be no trouble in recognizing what nouns they refer back to:

João está aqui mas *o seu* amigo está no Rio.
John is here but *his* friend is in Rio.

Os rapazes estão em Coimbra mas *o seu* amigo está em Lisboa.
The boys are in Coimbra but *their* friend is in Lisbon.

It is possible, however, to avoid any possible ambiguity by using the forms *dele* (his), *dela* (her), *deles* (their, referring to masculine possessors), *delas* (their, referring to feminine possessors), *do senhor* (your, referring to a masculine singular possessor), *da senhora* (your, referring to a feminine singular possessor), *dos senhores* (your, referring to masculine possessors) and *das senhoras* (your, referring to feminine possessors).* These forms follow the noun they accompany:

João está aqui mas o amigo *dele* está no Rio.
John is here but *his* friend is in Rio.

Os rapazes estão em Coimbra mas o amigo *deles* está em Lisboa.
The boys are in Coimbra but *their* friend is in Lisbon.

O livro *do senhor* está aí mas *os dela* estão aqui.
Your book is there but *hers* are here.

3. The definite article is omitted:

(a) before unmodified words of family relationship:†

Meu pai é velho.	*Nossos* tios estão alegres.
My father is old.	*Our* uncles are cheerful.

---

* The literal meaning of these forms is *of him, of her, of them* (masc.), *of them* (fem.), *of the gentleman, of the lady, of the gentlemen, of the ladies,* respectively.

† The article is not omitted when the forms *dele, dela,* etc., are employed.

(b) after the word *este* and after numerals:

Este meu livro é azul.
[This my book is blue.]
This book of mine is blue.

Dois amigos meus estão ali.
[Two friends mine are there.]
Two friends of mine are there.

(c) generally when the possessive stands alone:

De quem é este cão? É *meu*.
[Of whom is this dog? Is mine.]
Whose dog is this? It's *mine*.

Aquele automóvel é *nosso*.
That automobile is *ours*.

(d) There is a tendency (mainly in Brazil) to omit the article before a possessive that is used as an adjective:

Tenho *o meu* livro.   OR   Tenho *meu* livro.
I have *my* book.

However, the article is always used before a possessive that has the force of a pronoun:

Não tenho a minha gramática mas o Sr. tem *a sua*.
I do not have my grammar but you have *yours*.

4. Sometimes, contrary to English usage, the possessive adjective itself is omitted. This happens especially with parts of the body or with articles of clothing about whose ownership there can be no doubt.

Perdi *as* luvas.	Cortei *a* mão.
[I lost *the* gloves.]	[I cut *the* hand.]
I lost *my* gloves.	I cut *my* hand.

5. The form *o teu* (*a tua, os teus, as tuas*) is used only in conversation with relatives, close friends, etc., and should in general be avoided by the tourist. It is used less in Brazil than in Portugal. The form *o vosso*, etc., is now rare in both countries. To express "your," use the forms *o seu* (*a sua, os seus, as suas*) or *do senhor* (*da senhora*, etc.).

DEMONSTRATIVE ADJECTIVES
AND PRONOUNS

Demonstrative Adjectives

The demonstrative adjectives *este** (this), *esse* (that) and *aquele* (that) refer, as in English, to both persons and things. They always agree in gender and number with the noun they accompany:

MASC. SING.	FEM. SING.	MASC. PL.	FEM. PL.	
este	esta	estes	estas	this, these
esse	essa	esses	essas	that, those
aquele	aquela	aqueles	aquelas	that, those

The difference between the two words for "that" is that *esse* indicates something near the person being spoken to, while *aquele* indicates something further removed from both the speaker and the person addressed.

Esta casa é branca.
This house is white.

Estas casas são brancas.
These houses are white.

Esse cão é feroz.
That dog [near you] is fierce.

Esses cães são ferozes.
Those dogs [near you] are fierce.

Aquela montanha é alta.
That mountain [over there] is high.

Aquelas montanhas são altas.
Those mountains [over there] are high.

Contraction of Prepositions with *Este, Esse* and *Aquele*

The very common Portuguese prepositions *de* (of, from) and *em* (on, in) form contractions when used together with the demonstrative adjectives. The preposition *a* (to, at) contracts only with *aquele*:

* See second footnote on p. 9.

	MASC. SING.	FEM. SING.	MASC. PL.	FEM. PL.	
de + este	deste	desta	destes	destas	of this, of these
de + esse	desse	dessa	desses	dessas	of that, of those
de + aquele	daquele	daquela	daqueles	daquelas	of that, of those
em + este	neste	nesta	nestes	nestas	in this, in these
em + esse	nesse	nessa	nesses	nessas	in that, in those
em + aquele	naquele	naquela	naqueles	naquelas	in that, in those
a + aquele	àquele	àquela	àqueles	àquelas	to that, to those

O livro *deste* rapaz está *nessa* mala.
[The book *of this* boy is *in that* suitcase (near you).]
This boy's book is in that suitcase.

Dê o dinheiro *àquelas* mulheres.
Give the money *to those* women.

Este, Esse and Aquele as Pronouns

When used as pronouns (that is, without an accompanying noun), *este* means "this" or "this one," *esse* means "that" or "that one" (near you) and *aquele* means "that" or "that one" (over there). They can refer to both persons and things.*

Veja as duas mesas. *Esta* é mais bonita que *aquela*.
Look at the two tables. *This one* is nicer than *that one*.

Que sapatos prefere sua filha? *Esses*.
Which shoes does your daughter prefer? *Those*.

* To express "that of" or "those of" in Portuguese, the definite article is often used instead of the demonstratives:
As festas de Portugal e *as* do Brasil são magníficas.
The festivals of Portugal and *those* of Brazil are magnificent.

O chapéu dela e *o* de sua tia são novos.
[The hat of her and *that* of her aunt are new.]
Her hat and her aunt's are new.

The Pronouns *Isto, Isso* and *Aquilo*

The pronouns *isto* (this, this thing), *isso* (that, that thing [near you]) and *aquilo* (that, that thing [over there]) are used when referring to facts, ideas, vaguely identified objects, etc.; they never refer to persons.

Que é *isto*?
What is *this*?

Isso não tem importância.
[That not has importance.]
That does not matter.

Que é *aquilo* acolá?
What is *that thing* over there?

The preposition *de* contracts with *isto, isso* and *aquilo* to give *disto, disso* and *daquilo*, respectively. Contraction with *em* gives *nisto, nisso, naquilo*. The preposition *a* contracted with *aquilo* gives *àquilo*.

PERSONAL PRONOUNS

Even in English, some pronouns have different forms according to their use in a sentence; for example, "he" and "she" are subject pronouns, while "him" and "her" are the corresponding object pronouns. The situation in Portuguese is similar, but there are more forms to remember.

Subject Pronouns

	SING.		PL.	
1ST PERS.	eu	I	nós	we
2ND PERS.	tu	you (fam.)	vós	you (fam.; now rare)
3RD PERS.	ele	he	eles	they (masc.)
	ela	she	elas	they (fem.)
	o senhor	you (polite masc.)	os senhores	you (polite masc.)
	a senhora	you (polite fem.)	as senhoras	you (polite fem.)
	você	you (fam. masc. or fem.)	vocês	you (fam. masc. or fem.)

Observations on subject pronouns:

1. The Portuguese pronouns which correspond to the English "you" are *tu, vós, o senhor* (etc.), *você* and *vocês*. *Tu* is used in addressing members of the family, small children and close friends (compare the possessive adjective *o teu*). It is used less in Brazil than in Portugal. The use of *vós* (and the possessive *o vosso*) is today practically confined to sermons, political speeches and other formal public situations. *Você* is generally used in Brazil in the same situations of familiar address where *tu* is used in Portugal. In both Portugal and Brazil, *vocês* is used as the plural "you" in these familiar situations (addressing relatives, close friends, children, etc.). The polite form of "you" used in most situations and the one on which the tourist

34

should concentrate is *o senhor* (*a senhora, os senhores, as senhoras*), commonly abbreviated *o Sr.* (*a Sra., os Srs., as Sras.*). Even though *o senhor* (etc.) means "you," the verb that follows it is in the third person* (and the corresponding possessive is *o seu*).

2. Since Portuguese verbs have endings that indicate the person, it is not always necessary to use the subject pronoun with verbs as in English. The English subject pronoun "it" is very rarely expressed.

Sempre viajamos de carro.	Fala português?
We always travel by car.	Do you speak Portuguese?

Direct and Indirect Object Pronouns

In English the object pronouns (me, you, him, her, it, us, them) are either direct (He takes *it*) or indirect (He gives *me* the book, i.e., He gives the book *to me*). The same is true in Portuguese, except that in several cases object pronouns have a different form when they are direct and when they are indirect. Compare the two tables:

	DIRECT OBJECT PRONOUNS		INDIRECT OBJECT PRONOUNS
SING.			
1st pers.	me	me	me (to) me
2nd pers.	te	you (familiar)	te (to) you (fam.)
3rd pers.	o	him, it (masc.), you (polite masc.)	lhe (to) him, her, it (masc. or fem.), you (pol. masc. or fem.)
	a	her, it (fem.), you (pol. fem.)	
o senhor	you (pol. masc.)		ao senhor (to) you (pol. masc.)
a senhora	you (pol. fem.)		à senhora (to) you (pol. fem.)
você	you (fam. masc. or fem.)		a você (to) you (fam. masc. or fem.)

* The same is true of *você* and *vocês* and of some other more rarely used polite forms of "you."

DIRECT OBJECT PRONOUNS			INDIRECT OBJECT PRONOUNS	
PL.				
1st pers.	nos	us	nos	(to) us
2nd pers.	vos	you (formal fam.)	vos	(to) you (formal fam.)
3rd pers.	os	them (masc.), you (pol. masc.)	lhes	(to) them (masc. or fem.), you (pol. masc. or fem.)
	as	them (fem.), you (pol. fem.)		
os senhores		you (pol. masc.)	aos senhores	(to) you (pol. masc.)
as senhoras		you (pol. fem.)	às senhoras	(to) you (pol. fem.)
vocês		you (fam. masc. or fem.)	a vocês	(to) you (fam. masc. or fem.)

Ela deu-*me* o jornal. (indir. obj.)
She gave *me* the newspaper.

O Sr. *o* viu ontem. (dir. obj.)
You saw *him* yesterday.

      (dir. obj.)   (indir. obj.)
Agora não *a* vejo, mas *lhe* falei às sete horas.
Now I don't see *her*, but I spoke *to her* at seven o'clock.

Observations:

1. In general, Portuguese direct and indirect object pronouns may precede or follow the verb.   When they follow, they are connected to the verb by a hyphen.

João *me* vê.   OR   João vê-*me*.
John sees *me*.

But the object pronoun cannot be the first word in a sentence:

Vê-*me*. (no other word order possible).
He sees *me*.

2. The object pronouns precede the verb in a negative sentence:
Não *me* moleste.   (no other word order possible)
Don't annoy *me*.

3. The polite forms of "you" (dir. obj.) and "to you" on which you should concentrate are *o* (you, masc. sing.), *a* (you, fem. sing.), *os* (you, masc. pl.), *as* (you, fem. pl.), *lhe* (to you, masc. or fem. sing.) and *lhes* (to you, masc. or fem. pl.). It is also possible (especially to avoid confusion with the other meanings of *o, a, os, as*) to express "you" by *o senhor* (masc. sing.), *a senhora* (fem. sing.), *os senhores* (masc. pl.), *as senhoras* (fem. pl.) and "to you" by *ao senhor* (masc. sing.), *à senhora* (fem. sing.), *aos senhores* (masc. pl.), *às senhoras* (fem. pl.). These longer forms always follow the verb; no hyphen is used.

Vejo-*o*.   OR   Vejo *o senhor* (*o Sr.*).
I see *you*.

Não *lhes* dou o dinheiro.   OR   Não dou o dinheiro *às se-*
                                       nhoras (*às Sras.*).
I am not giving *you* the money.

4. When the object pronouns *o, a, os, as* follow a verb form ending in *-r, -z* or *-s*, they become *lo, la, los, las*, and the *-r, -z* or *-s* is dropped:

Faz ele o trabalho? Fá-*lo*.   (faz+o)
Does he do the work? He does *it*.

Há lições para estudar.   Vamos estudá-*las*.   (estudar+as)
There are lessons to study.   Let's study *them*.

When *o, a, os, as* follow a verb form ending in *-m* or *-ão*, they become *no, na, nos, nas*:

Falam eles português?   Falam-*no*.   (falam+o)
Do they speak Portuguese?   They speak *it*.

Dão elas as luvas ao rapaz?   Não, dão-*nas* à mãe dele.   (dão+as)
Are they giving the gloves to the boy?   No, they are giving *them* to his mother.

You can usually avoid these more difficult situations by placing *o, a, os, as* before the verb (when this is possible) or by avoiding the use of those pronouns as explained on page 39.

Direct and Indirect Object Pronouns with the Same Verb

When a verb has both a direct and an indirect object pronoun, the indirect precedes the direct.   When the direct object pronouns used are *o, a, os, as*, they combine with the indirect object pronouns as follows:

INDIR. OBJ. PRON.	+o	+a	+os	+as
me	mo	ma	mos	mas
te	to	ta	tos	tas
lhe	lho	lha	lhos	lhas
nos	no-lo*	no-la	no-los	no-las
vos	vo-lo*	vo-la	vo-los	vo-las
lhes	lho	lha	lhos	lhas

Diz-*mo*.
He tells *it* *to me*.

Prefere estas luvas?   Vendo-*lhas* muito barato.
Do you prefer these gloves?   I (shall) sell *them* *to you* very cheap.

(See the section below on how to avoid the use of double pronouns.)

Stressed (Prepositional) Forms of the Personal Pronouns

These are the pronouns used after prepositions:

SING.		PL.	
para *mim*	for *me*	atrás de *nós*	behind *us*
sem *ti*	without *you* (fam.)	perto de *vós*	near *you* (formal fam.)
com *ele*	with *him*	contra *eles*	against *them* (masc.)
a *ela*	to *her*	entre *elas*	among *them* (fem.)
com *o senhor*	with *you* (polite masc.)	com *os senhores*	with *you* (polite masc.)
para *a senhora*	for *you* (polite fem.)	sem *as senhoras*	without *you* (polite fem.)
sem *você*	without *you* (fam. masc. or fem.)	a *vocês*	to *you* (fam. masc. or fem.)

The preposition *com* (with) makes the following irregular combinations: *comigo* (with me), *contigo* (with you [fam. sing.]) *consigo* (with himself, herself, itself; with themselves; with yourself, yourselves [pol.]), *connosco* (with us), *convosco* (with you [formal fam. pl.]).

* The combinations with *nos* and *vos* are almost always avoided in conversation.

How to Avoid the Use of Double Pronouns

You can avoid object pronouns (I showed *them* to *him*) by replacing them with nouns (I showed *the pictures* to *James*). You can avoid using two pronouns with the same verb by replacing one of them with a noun (I showed *them* to *James*).

Deu-*mo*. (2 obj. prons.)	Deu-*me* o livro. (1 obj. pron.)
He gave *it to me*.	He gave *me* the book.
Não *lhas* dê. (2 obj. prons.)	Não *lhe* dê as cartas. (1 obj. pron.)
Don't give *them to her*.	Don't give *her* the cards.

Instead of the indirect object pronoun you can use the stressed form of the pronoun with the preposition *a* (to). In this way you avoid combinations such as *mo*, *lhas*, etc., and escape any possible ambiguity among the various meanings of *lhe* and *lhes*.

Deu-*mo*.	Deu-*o a mim*.
He gave *it to me*.	He gave *it to me*.
Não *lhas* dê.	Não *as* dê *a ela*.
Don't give *them to her*.	Don't give *them to her*.

Table of Personal Pronouns

You will find the following table useful in reviewing the personal pronouns. For the sake of completeness we are including the *reflexive pronouns* here too. You will need to know them when you study reflexive verbs on page 68.

TABLE OF PRONOUNS

| | | UNSTRESSED | | | STRESSED |
| | | OBJECT | | | (PREPOSITIONAL)* |
SUBJECT		DIRECT	INDIRECT	REFLEXIVE	
SING. 1st pers.	eu I	me me	me to me	me myself, to myself	mim me
2nd pers.	tu you (fam.)	te you	te to you	te yourself, to yourself	ti you
3rd pers.	ele he	o him, it	lhe to him, it	se himself, herself, itself, to himself, etc.	ele him
	ela she	a her, it	lhe to her, it		ela her
					si himself, herself, itself
	o senhor you (polite masc.)	o OR you / o senhor	lhe OR to you / ao senhor	se yourself, to yourself	o senhor you
	a senhora you (polite fem.)	a OR you / a senhora	lhe OR to you / à senhora	se yourself, to yourself	a senhora you
					si yourself
	você you (fam. masc. and fem.)	você you	a você to you	se yourself, to yourself	você you
					si yourself

* For special forms of pronouns with the preposition *com*, see page 38.

		UNSTRESSED			STRESSED (PREPOSITIONAL)
	SUBJECT	OBJECT			
		DIRECT	INDIRECT	REFLEXIVE	
PL. 1st pers.	nós we	nos us	nos to us	nos ourselves, to ourselves	nós us
2nd pers.	vós you (formal fam.)	vos you	vos to you	vos yourselves, to yourselves	vós you
3rd pers.	eles they (masc.)	os them	lhes to them	se themselves, to themselves	eles them
	elas they (fem.)	as them	lhes to them		elas them
					si themselves
	os senhores you (polite masc.)	os OR you os senhores	lhes OR to you aos senhores	se yourselves, to yourselves	os senhores you
	as senhoras you (polite fem.)	as OR you as senhoras	lhes OR to you às senhoras	se yourselves, to yourselves	as senhoras you
					si yourselves
	vocês you (fam. masc. and fem.)	vocês you	a vocês to you	se yourselves, to yourselves	vocês you
					si yourselves

NEGATIVES

In Portuguese any sentence can be made negative by placing *não* (not) before the verb:

Esta cidade *não* é muito grande.
This city is *not* very large.

Não falo muito bem.
[Not I speak very well.]
I do *not* speak very well.

If the verb has an object pronoun, this pronoun comes between the *não* and the verb:

Não o vejo.
[*Not* him I see.]
I don't see him.

Other important negatives are:

ninguém	nobody
nenhum, nenhuma, nenhuns, nenhumas	no, none (adjective)
nada	nothing
nem . . . nem	neither . . . nor
nunca	never
nunca mais	never again

1. When these negatives follow the verb, *não* is placed before the verb:

Não está aqui *ninguém*.
[Not is here nobody.]
Nobody is here.

Ele *não* tem *nenhum* dinheiro.
[He *not* has *no* money.]
He has no money.

42

Não tenho *nada.*
[*Not* I have *nothing.*]
I have nothing.　OR　I don't have anything.

2. When one of these negatives precedes the verb, it is not followed by another negative:

Nem João *nem* Maria sabe nadar.
Neither John *nor* Mary knows (how) to swim.

Ele *nunca* vem.
He *never* comes.

QUE AS CONJUNCTION AND RELATIVE PRONOUN

Que as Conjunction

In English the conjunction *that* is frequently omitted. (*I know that I am right* is often abbreviated to *I know I am right*.) In Portuguese the conjunction *que* must be expressed.

Sei *que* ela vem.
I know (*that*) she is coming.

Jorge diz *que* seu irmão é rico.
George says (*that*) his brother is rich.

Que as Relative Pronoun

In addition to being a conjunction (and an interrogative, see p. 10), *que* is also a relative pronoun (*who, which, that, whom*). It refers to either persons or things, singular or plural, masculine or feminine, and can be used as either subject or object. It is the most important of the relative pronouns.

Ele é o mesmo rapaz *que* veio a semana passada. (refers to a person, subject)
He is the same boy *who* came last week.

Desejo um chapéu *que* não custe demais. (refers to a thing, subject)
I want a hat *that* does not cost too much.

As mulheres *que* o senhor procura não estão aqui. (refers to persons, object)
The women *whom* you are looking for are not here.

Onde estão os sapatos *que* comprei em Lisboa? (refers to things, object)
Where are the shoes *which* I bought in Lisbon?

Observations:

1. After prepositions, "whom" is translated as *quem*:
   Os estudantes de *quem* fala são americanos.
   The students of *whom* he is speaking (or, whom he is speaking about) are Americans.

2. The relative pronoun "what" (I know *what* I am doing) is translated as *o que*:
   Não me diz nunca *o que* faz.
   He never tells me *what* he is doing.

3. The relative pronoun "whose" is translated as *cujo* (*cuja, cujos, cujas*). Unlike the other relative words we have discussed, *cujo* agrees in gender and number with the noun that follows it:
   A mulher *cujos* filhos estão doentes está muito preocupada.
   The woman *whose* children are ill is very worried.

4. You will notice that in most cases Portuguese has different equivalents for the *relative* words "who," "which," "what," "whose" and the *interrogative* "who," "which," "what," "whose" (discussed on page 10). You should be careful not to confuse them. Also, do not confuse the relative pronoun and conjunction "that" with the demonstrative adjective and pronoun "that" (discussed on pages 31 to 33).

PREPOSITIONS

Some important prepositions that have not occurred earlier in this book are:

antes de, before	Veio a Lisboa *antes da* guerra.
	He came to Lisbon *before the* war.
após, after	Um *após* outro entraram na classe.
	One *after* the other they entered the class.
depois de, after	Cheguei *depois de* meia-noite.
	I arrived *after* midnight.
até, until, as far as	A estrada vai *até* o Porto.
	The road goes *as far as* Oporto.
desde, since	Não o vi *desde* Agosto.
	I haven't seen him *since* August.
através de, through, across	Viagei *através da* América.
	I traveled *across* America.
sob, under	O gato está *sob* a mesa.
	The cat is *under* the table.
sobre, over, on	O livro está *sobre* a cadeira.
	The book is *on* the chair.
por cima de, over, above	O avião passou *por cima da* cidade.
	The plane passed *over the* city.
ao lado de, beside	Há uma árvore alta *ao lado da* casa.
	There is a tall tree *beside the* house.

Por and Para

The prepositions *por* and *para* have both appeared in this book translated as "for," but they have different shades of meaning and are not interchangeable. *Por* is used when "for" means "for the sake of," "on account of" or "in exchange for." *Para* indicates destination or purpose. Study the following examples. (Remember that *por* contracts with the definite article, giving *pelo, pela, pelos, pelas*!)

46

Ele lutou *pela* pátria.
[He fought *for the* country.]
He fought for his country.

Quanto pagou o senhor *pelos* sapatos?
How much did you pay *for the* shoes?

Este regalo é *para* o Joãozinho.
This present is *for* little Johnny.

Partimos logo *para* os Estados Unidos.
We are leaving at once *for* the United States.

Both these prepositions are frequently employed with other meanings. *Por* may often be translated as "through" or "by," *para* as "to" or "toward."

Olhei *pela* janela mas não vi nada.
I looked *through the* window but I saw nothing.

Foi acusado *por* um desconhecido.
He was accused *by* a stranger.

Vamos *para* o jardim.
Let's go *to* the garden.

Não tenho bastante tempo *para* estudar.
I don't have enough time *to* study.

The differences between these two prepositions can sometimes be very subtle, but as a beginner in Portuguese you will probably find the basic distinctions presented here perfectly adequate.

CONJUNCTIONS

Although we are emphasizing simple, straightforward expressions, there will be need from time to time to use longer, more complicated sentences. For this purpose you should become acquainted with the following list of basic conjunctions.

e	and	Chegámos tarde demais *e* não achámos um quarto no hotel. We arrived too late *and* didn't find a room in the hotel.
ou	or	Deseja ir ao cinema *ou* prefere o teatro? Do you want to go to the movies *or* do you prefer the theater?
mas	but	Esperei todo o dia *mas* ninguém veio. I waited all day *but* nobody came.
quando	when	Fico triste *quando* chove. I am sad *when* it rains.
enquanto que	while	*Enquanto que* estive fora, um ladrão entrou na casa. *While* I was out, a thief entered the house.
se	if	*Se* é verdade, é uma boa notícia. *If* it is true, it is a good piece of news.
porque	because	Não o fazem *porque* não podem. They aren't doing it *because* they can't.
ainda que	although, even if (usually followed by subjunctive)	*Ainda que* venha cedo, não me achará em casa. *Even if* you come early, you won't find me at home.

48

VERBS

Before proceeding to study this section, you should become acquainted with the material covered in pages 102 to 105 of the Glossary of Grammatical Terms. Although you may not remember everything at a first reading, this material will help you to understand special constructions and expressions as you come to them.

Comparison of English and Portuguese Verbs

Portuguese verbs are more complicated than English ones. In English there are very few changes in endings, and those that do occur are relatively uniform: I walk, he walks; I hope, he hopes. In Portuguese, each person has its own distinctive ending: eu falo (*I* speak), o senhor fala (*you* speak). Since the subject pronoun is very often omitted in Portuguese, failure to employ the correct ending results in misunderstanding: falo (*I* speak), fala (*you* speak).

Another aspect in which Portuguese verbs are more complicated than English is the greater number of tenses used in Portuguese. You will notice this when we speak of the various past tenses and of the subjunctive mood. Though it is possible to avoid some difficulties by using short, simple sentences, it is necessary to be acquainted with the various features of the Portuguese verb for understanding the spoken and the written language. In the pages which follow, we shall always distinguish between those forms which must be memorized from the start and those which you can study at a later date.

The Three Conjugations

Every Portuguese verb belongs to one of three conjugations. Since the various endings which a particular verb takes are determined by the conjugation to which it belongs, you must pay special attention to this point. By classifying verbs into conjugations it is easier to remember their many forms.

The conjugation to which a Portuguese verb belongs is determined by the ending of its infinitive (that is, of the form which corresponds to the English "to run," "to believe," etc.).

Verbs ending in -*ar* belong to the *first conjugation*
" " " -*er* " " " *second conjugation*
" " " -*ir* " " " *third conjugation*

All verbs which belong to the same conjugation (except irregular ones) are conjugated like the model verb of that conjugation. Our model verbs are:

falar (to speak)   *first conjugation*
vender (to sell)   *second conjugation*
partir (to depart)   *third conjugation*

Regular verbs ending in -*ar* will therefore take the same endings as the model verb *falar*. Regular verbs in -*er* and -*ir* will take the same endings as the models *vender* and *partir*, respectively.

Irregular verbs will be treated separately in Appendix D.

The Present Tense

Comparison of Present Tense in English and Portuguese

In English we have three different ways of expressing an action in the present. We can say "I laugh," "I am laughing" or "I do laugh." The three forms are distinguished by slight differences in meaning. In Portuguese, on the other hand, a single present tense conveys all three meanings of the English.

First Conjugation

Memorize the present tense of the model verb *falar* (to speak):

(eu)	fal*o*	I speak, am speaking, do speak
(tu)	fal*as*	you (fam. sing.) speak, are speaking, do speak
(ele)	fal*a*	he (she, it) speaks, is speaking, does speak; you (polite sing.) speak, are speaking, do speak*
(nós)	fal*amos*	we speak, are speaking, do speak
(vós)	fal*ais*	you (formal fam. pl.) speak, are speaking, do speak

* This would be a good occasion to review the subject pronouns (p. 34), especially the polite forms of "you," which take the *third* person of the verb.

(eles) fal*am*   they speak, are speaking, do speak; you (polite pl.) speak, are speaking, do speak

Second Conjugation

Memorize the present tense of the model verb *vender* (to sell):

(eu)   vend*o*   I sell, am selling, do sell
(tu)   vend*es*   you (fam. sing.) sell, are selling, do sell
(ele)   vend*e*   he (she, it) sells, is selling, does sell; you (polite sing.) sell, are selling, do sell
(nós)   vend*emos*   we sell, are selling, do sell
(vós)   vend*eis*   you (formal fam. pl.) sell, are selling, do sell
(eles)   vend*em*   they sell, are selling, do sell; you (polite pl.) sell, are selling, do sell

Third Conjugation

Memorize the present tense of the model verb *partir* (to depart):

(eu)   part*o*   I depart, am departing, do depart
(tu)   part*es*   you (fam. sing.) depart, are departing, do depart
(ele)   part*e*   he (she, it) departs, is departing, does depart; you (polite sing.) depart, are departing, do depart
(nós)   part*imos*   we depart, are departing, do depart
(vós)   part*is*   you (formal fam. pl.) depart, are departing, do depart
(eles)   part*em*   they depart, are departing, do depart; you (polite pl.) depart, are departing, do depart

Observations on the present tense:

1. If you prefer, you may omit the *tu*-form and the *vós*-form in memorizing, since as a tourist you will not be likely to use them.

2. To help you remember the endings of the present tense for the three conjugations note that:

(a) in all three conjugations, the first person singular ends in -*o*.
(b) the first person plural ending has the characteristic vowel of the infinitive: fal*a*mos, vend*e*mos, part*i*mos, but is otherwise the same in all three conjugations.

(c) in the second and third conjugations, all endings are alike except for the *nós*- and *vós*-forms: vend*emos*, vend*eis*; part*imos*, part*is*.

For the present tense of irregular verbs see Appendix D. Appendixes B and C contain further information on the present tense of certain types of regular verbs.

The Progressive Present

In studying the present tense you no doubt noticed that *falo* was translated both as "I speak" and as "I am speaking." The form "I am speaking" is more vivid than "I speak" because the action is represented as going on, as being in progress. However, there is no time difference between the two forms, so that we can say either "The train arrives" or "The train is arriving" and refer to exactly the same time. Both in English and Portuguese, the present participle (the verb form ending in *-ing*: "running," "waiting") is used in forming the progressive.*

The Present Participle

In Portuguese, the present participle (also called gerund) is formed by dropping the infinitive ending *-ar*, *-er*, *-ir*, and adding *-ando* to verbs of the first conjugation, *-endo* to verbs of the second conjugation and *-indo* to verbs of the third conjugation. These endings never change.

fal*ar* (to speak)	fal*ando* (speaking)
vend*er* (to sell)	vend*endo* (selling)
part*ir* (to depart)	part*indo* (departing)

The Use of *Estar.*

Of the two Portuguese verbs which mean "to be," the one which is used in forming the progressive is *estar.*†

Estou escrevendo‡ uma carta.	*I am writing* a letter.
O comboio está chegando.	The train *is arriving.*
De quem está falando?	Of whom *are you speaking?*

---

* The progressive present is not as frequent in Portuguese as in English. For instance, in Portuguese it cannot be used as the equivalent of an English sentence like "I am leaving tomorrow," where the future is implied. In such cases, use the simple present or the future tense in Portuguese.

† Other differences in the use of *ser* and *estar* will be discussed on page 75.

‡ Also *Estou a escrever.* This form is more frequently used in Portugal.

The Imperative or Command Form

To distinguish between the different verb forms used for giving commands, we must go back to the different pronouns which all mean "you" in Portuguese: *tu, o senhor (a senhora), você, vós, os senhores (as senhoras), vocês*. Since you will be using the polite forms (*o senhor, etc.*) most frequently, we shall study them first. Concentrate on the singular.

Polite Command Forms (Third Person Forms)

falar (to speak)	fal*e* (polite sing.)—speak!
	fal*em* (polite pl.)—speak!
vender (to sell)	vend*a* (polite sing.)—sell!
	vend*am* (polite pl.)—sell!
partir (to depart)	part*a* (polite sing.)—depart!
	part*am* (polite pl.)—depart!

Irregular command forms are discussed in Appendix D. Appendixes B and C give further details for certain regular verbs.

To soften a command add one of the expressions *por favor* or *faça favor* ("please"):

Abra a janela, *faça favor.*   Open the window, *please.*
Por favor, dê-me um copo de água.   *Please* give me a glass of water.

To avoid the command form altogether use the expressions *Faça favor de* ("Do [me] the favor of") or *Queira* ("Be willing to") with the infinitive. With *Queira*, it is a good idea to add *por favor* in order to soften the command.

Faça favor de abrir a janela.
Queira abrir a janela, *por favor.*
Please open the window.

First Person Plural Commands

The most common and convenient way to express the first person plural command ("Let's hurry!" "Let's stop!") in Portuguese is to use *Vamos* plus the infinitive of the verb:

Vamos falar com o capitão.   *Let's talk* to the captain.
Vamos visitar o museu.   *Let's visit* the museum.

Vamos alone means "Let's go!"

Vamos para o jardim.   *Let's go* to the garden.

Another form of the first person plural command is arrived at by dropping the endings (-*e*, -*em* for the first conjugation; -*a*, -*am* for the rest) of the *polite command form*, and adding -*emos* for first conjugation verbs and -*amos* for all others.

INFINITIVE	POLITE COMMAND FORMS	"LET'S" COMMAND FORM
falar (to speak)	fal*e*, fal*em*	fal*emos* (let's speak)
vender (to sell)	vend*a*, vend*am*	vend*amos* (let's sell)
partir (to depart)	part*a*, part*am*	part*amos* (let's depart)

Familiar Command Forms

The command forms for *tu* and *vós* are as follows for the three regular conjugations:

falar (to speak)	fala (fam. sing.)—speak!
	falai (formal fam. pl.)—speak!
vender (to sell)	vende (fam. sing.)—sell!
	vendei (formal fam. pl.)—sell!
partir (to depart)	parte (fam. sing.)—depart!
	parti (formal fam. pl.)—depart!

Review Table of Command Forms (Regular Conjugations)

	FIRST CONJUGATION	SECOND CONJUGATION	THIRD CONJUGATION
(fam. sing.)	fala	vende	parte
(polite sing.)	fale	venda	parta
(first person pl.)	vamos falar	vamos vender	vamos partir
	OR falemos	OR vendamos	OR partamos
(formal fam. pl.)	falai	vendei	parti
(polite pl.)	falem	vendam	partam

The Past Definite Tense

In Portuguese, as in English, there are several tenses to express what happened in the past. The most widely used past tense in Portuguese is the past definite, or preterit, which corresponds in meaning to the simple English past: "I slept," "I left," "I sold," and in most cases also to the English present perfect: "I have slept," "I have left," "I have sold."*

* For the Portuguese present perfect tense and its limited use, see Appendix A.

The Past Definite of the Model Verbs

FIRST CONJUGATION

falei	I spoke, have spoken
falaste	you (fam. sing.) spoke, have spoken
falou	he (she, it) spoke, has spoken; you (polite sing.) spoke, have spoken
falámos	we spoke, have spoken
falastes	you (formal fam. pl.) spoke, have spoken
falaram	they spoke, have spoken; you (polite pl.) spoke, have spoken

SECOND CONJUGATION

vendi	I sold, have sold
vendeste	you (fam. sing.) sold, have sold
vendeu	he (she, it) sold, has sold; you (polite sing.) sold, have sold
vendemos	we sold, have sold
vendestes	you (formal fam. pl.) sold, have sold
venderam	they sold, have sold; you (polite pl.) sold, have sold

THIRD CONJUGATION

parti	I departed, have departed
partiste	you (fam. sing.) departed, have departed
partiu	he (she, it) departed, has departed; you (polite sing.) departed, have departed
partimos	we departed, have departed
partistes	you (formal fam. pl.) departed, have departed
partiram	they departed, have departed; you (polite pl.) departed, have departed

Observations on the past definite of the model verbs:

You have probably noticed that the characteristic conjugation vowel (*a* for verbs ending in -*ar*; *e* for verbs ending in -*er*; *i* for verbs ending in -*ir*) appears in every form of the past definite, except in the first person singular of the first and second conjugations and the third person singular of the first conjugation. Aside from the conjugation vowel, the endings in the three conjugations are identical (fal*aste*, vend*este*, part*iste*).

For the past definite of irregular verbs see Appendix D. Appendix B contains further details on certain regular verbs.

The Imperfect Tense

The imperfect tense is used to tell what was happening or what used to happen in the past. It is also the tense of description in the past. It is extremely simple to conjugate a verb in the imperfect tense, since only four verbs have irregular forms (see Appendix D). The forms of the first person singular and third person singular are always identical. The second and third conjugations have the same endings throughout.

The Imperfect Tense of the Model Verbs

FIRST CONJUGATION

falava	I spoke, used to speak, was speaking
falavas	you (fam. sing.) spoke, used to speak, were speaking
falava	he (she, it) spoke, used to speak, was speaking; you (polite sing.) spoke, used to speak, were speaking
falávamos	we spoke, used to speak, were speaking
faláveis	you (formal fam. pl.) spoke, used to speak, were speaking
falavam	they spoke, used to speak, were speaking; you (polite pl.) spoke, used to speak, were speaking

SECOND CONJUGATION

vendia	I sold, used to sell, was selling
vendias	you (fam. sing.) sold, used to sell, were selling
vendia	he (she, it) sold, used to sell, was selling; you (polite sing.) sold, used to sell, were selling
vendíamos	we sold, used to sell, were selling
vendíeis	you (formal fam. pl.) sold, used to sell, were selling
vendiam	they sold, used to sell, were selling; you (polite pl.) sold, used to sell, were selling

THIRD CONJUGATION

partia	I departed, used to depart, was departing
partias	you (fam. sing.) departed, used to depart, were departing
partia	he (she, it) departed, used to depart, was departing; you (polite sing.) departed, used to depart, were departing
partíamos	we departed, used to depart, were departing

| partíeis | you (formal fam. pl.) departed, used to depart, were departing |
| partiam | they departed, used to depart, were departing; you (polite pl.) departed, used to depart, were departing |

The Uses of the Imperfect Tense

The following sentences illustrate the differences in use between the imperfect and the past definite tenses. Generally speaking, the *imperfect* is the tense used to describe something in the past, or to refer to something which used to happen or was happening in the past. The *past definite* refers to a single completed action which happened at some definite time in the past.

Eu *falava* a João todos os dias. [I used to speak to John all the days.]	I *used to speak* to John every day.
Eu *falei* a João ontem.	I *spoke* to John yesterday.
Nós *líamos* quando ele *chegou.*	We *were reading* when he *arrived.*
Aonde *ia* o senhor quando o *vi?*	Where *were* you *going* when I *saw* you?
Ela *era* uma criança bonita quando *vivíamos* na casa de sua mãe.	She *was* a lovely child when we *lived* in her mother's house.

The imperfect is frequently used idiomatically in Portuguese in place of the conditional tense (see conditional, page 62):

Desejava ler este livro. (normally, *Desejaria*)
I would like to read this book.

Não sabia se eles *vinham.* (normally, *viriam*)
I didn't know whether they *would come.*

The Pluperfect Tense

The pluperfect tense is used in Portuguese, as in English, to refer to an action which *had* taken place prior to another action in the past. Portuguese forms the pluperfect in two altogether different ways. The type of pluperfect that is used almost exclusively in conversation—the one on which you should concentrate—is a compound tense, formed with the *imperfect* tense of the helping verb *ter** (or, less frequently, *haver*; both mean "to have") and the past participle.

The Past Participle

In Portuguese, the past participle is formed by dropping the infinitive ending *-ar*, *-er*, *-ir* and adding *-ado* to verbs of the first conjugation and *-ido* to verbs of the second and third conjugations:

fal*ar* (to speak)	fal*ado* (spoken)
vend*er* (to sell)	vend*ido* (sold)
part*ir* (to depart)	part*ido* (departed)

For irregular past participles see Appendix D.

The Pluperfect Tense (Compound Type) of the Model Verbs

FIRST CONJUGATION

tinha falado	I had spoken
tinhas falado	you (fam. sing.) had spoken
tinha falado	he (she, it) had spoken; you (polite sing.) had spoken
tínhamos falado	we had spoken
tínheis falado	you (formal fam. pl.) had spoken
tinham falado	they had spoken; you (polite pl.) had spoken

SECOND CONJUGATION

tinha vendido	I had sold
tinhas vendido	you (fam. sing.) had sold
tinha vendido	he (she, it) had sold; you (polite sing.) had sold
tínhamos vendido	we had sold
tínheis vendido	you (formal fam. pl.) had sold
tinham vendido	they had sold; you (polite pl.) had sold

THIRD CONJUGATION

tinha partido	I had departed
tinhas partido	you (fam. sing.) had departed
tinha partido	he (she, it) had departed; you (polite sing.) had departed
tínhamos partido	we had departed
tínheis partido	you (formal fam. pl.) had departed

* *Tinha, tinhas, tinha, tínhamos, tínheis, tinham.*

tinham partido   they had departed; you (polite pl.) had
                          departed

For the secondary pluperfect tense, which is almost never used in
conversation, see the full paradigm of regular verbs in Appendix A.

The Future Tense

The future tense (in English, *will* or *shall* plus the infinitive: "I
shall come") is formed by adding the endings *-ei, -ás, -á, -emos,- eis, -ão*
to the complete infinitive of the verb.

The Future Tense of the Model Verbs

FIRST CONJUGATION

falarei	I shall speak
falarás	you (fam. sing.) will speak
falará	he (she, it) will speak; you (polite sing.) will speak
falaremos	we shall speak
falareis	you (formal fam. pl.) will speak
falarão	they will speak; you (polite pl.) will speak

SECOND CONJUGATION

venderei	I shall sell
venderás	you (fam. sing.) will sell
venderá	he (she, ít) will sell; you (polite sing.) will sell
venderemos	we shall sell
vendereis	you (formal fam. pl.) will sell
venderão	they will sell; you (polite pl.) will sell

THIRD CONJUGATION

partirei	I shall depart
partirás	you (fam. sing.) will depart
partirá	he (she, it) will depart; you (polite sing.) will depart
partiremos	we shall depart
partireis	you (formal fam. pl.) will depart
partirão	they will depart; you (polite pl.) will depart

Only three Portuguese verbs have an irregular future (see Appendix D).

The Uses of the Future Tense

Study the following sentences which illustrate the use of the future in Portuguese. In general, English and Portuguese use corresponds.

O que *fará* amanhã?	What *will you do* tomorrow?
Visitaremos uns amigos.	*We shall visit* some friends.
Estarão em casa amanhã?	*Will they be* at home tomorrow?

There is one use of the future in Portuguese which has no equivalent in English. The future can be used in Portuguese to express what is probable in the present.

Serão oito horas.	It is *probably* eight o'clock (OR
[*They will be* eight hours.]	It is *about* eight o'clock).
Será ele que fala.	It is *probably* he who is speaking.

Position of Object Pronouns with the Future Tense

It is incorrect in Portuguese to place a direct or indirect object after the entire future form of a verb; for instance, you should not say *venderei-o* for "I shall sell it." When the object pronoun does not precede the verb (as it does in *eu o venderei*, which is perfectly correct), or when some conversational substitute for the future tense is not employed (see below on how to avoid the future tense), the object pronoun must be placed between the two components of the future, that is, between the infinitive and the endings. Hyphens are placed between the infinitive and the pronoun and between the pronoun and the ending. The direct object pronouns *o, a, os* and *as* become *lo, la, los* and *las*, and the *-r* of the infinitive is dropped before these forms. We are showing this rather difficult arrangement of the object pronouns for the sake of completeness; you will come across it if you begin to read Portuguese. But it is to be avoided in conversation.* We shall show this arrangement in verbs of the three regular conjugations, first with the direct object pronoun *o* (which becomes *lo*) and then with the indirect object pronoun *lhe*.

WITH DIRECT OBJ.	WITH INDIRECT OBJ.
FIRST CONJUGATION	
procurar, to look for	*falar*, to speak
procurá-lo-ei (I shall look for it)	falar-lhe-ei (I shall speak to him)
procurá-lo-ás	falar-lhe-ás

* Use the form *eu o venderei*. Include the subject pronoun (*eu, o senhor*, etc.), because the object pronoun cannot begin a sentence.

procurá-lo-á

procurá-lo-emos

procurá-lo-eis

procurá-lo-ão

falar-lhe-á

falar-lhe-emos

falar-lhe-eis

falar-lhe-ão

SECOND CONJUGATION

aprender, to learn

aprendê-lo-ei (I shall learn it)

aprendê-lo-ás

aprendê-lo-á

aprendê-lo-emos

aprendê-lo-eis

aprendê-lo-ão

escrever, to write

escrever-lhe-ei (I shall write to him)

escrever-lhe-ás

escrever-lhe-á

escrever-lhe-emos

escrever-lhe-eis

escrever-lhe-ão

THIRD CONJUGATION

abrir, to open

abri-lo-ei (I shall open it)

abri-lo-ás

abri-lo-á

abri-lo-emos

abri-lo-eis

abri-lo-ão

repetir, to repeat

repetir-lhe-ei (I shall repeat to him)

repetir-lhe-ás

repetir-lhe-á

repetir-lhe-emos

repetir-lhe-eis

repetir-lhe-ão

How to Avoid the Future Tense

Conversational Portuguese commonly employs several easy and convenient substitutes for the future tense that convey the same meaning.

1. You can use the present tense of the (irregular) verb *ir* (to go) followed by the infinitive of the main verb. This is just like the English construction "I am going to speak."

Vou ver João esta tarde.   *I am going to see* John this afternoon (OR *I shall see* John this afternoon).

2. You can use the present tense of *ter* followed by *que* (or *de*) plus the infinitive of the main verb.

Temos que ver (or *Temos de ver*) João hoje.   *We shall see* John today.

3. You can use the present tense of *haver* followed by *de* (which is connected to the form of *haver* by a hyphen) plus the infinitive of the main verb.

Hei-de ver João amanhã.   *I shall see* John tomorrow.

For the *future perfect* tense see the full paradigm of regular verbs in Appendix A.

The Conditional Mood

The conditional (in English, *would* plus the infinitive) is formed by adding the endings *-ia, -ias, -ia, -íamos, -íeis, -iam* to the complete infinitive of the verb (as for the future tense).*

The Conditional of the Model Verb *Falar*

falaria	I would speak
falarias	you (fam. sing.) would speak
falaria	he (she, it) would speak; you (polite sing.) would speak
falaríamos	we would speak
falaríeis	you (formal fam. pl.) would speak
falariam	they would speak; you (polite pl.) would speak

For irregular verbs see Appendix D.

The Uses of the Conditional

The conditional is used in Portuguese as it is in English (I *would go*, if I could).

Não o faria.   *I would* not *do* it.

Gostaríamos de ir aos Açores.   *We would like* to go to the Azores.

See page 57 for the use of the imperfect in place of the conditional.

The conditional is also used, contrary to English, to express probability in the past (just as the future is used to express probability in the present; see page 60), or to express surprise or disbelief.

Seriam oito horas.   *It was probably* eight o'clock (OR
[*They would be* eight hours.]   *It was about* eight o'clock).

Seria ele que falava.   *It was probably* he who was speaking.

Seria verdade?   *Can it be* true?
[*Would it be* truth?]

---

* The use of object pronouns with the conditional is exactly the same as with the future tense (see discussion above, page 60).

For the formation of the *conditional perfect* tense see Appendix A.
A further discussion of the conditional in if-sentences will be found on page 67.

The Subjunctive Mood

The subjunctive, which survives in English in sentences such as "If I *were* to call him, he would come at once," occurs much more frequently in Portuguese. It is therefore important that you know something about it and that you be familiar with its forms.

With very few exceptions, the subjunctive occurs only in dependent clauses. Although it is usually possible to break up a long, complex sentence into two or more short, simple sentences, there are cases where this is impossible. Instead of saying, "Here is the chauffeur who drove us to the station," we can very well say, "Here is the chauffeur. He drove us to the station." But how else can we express ideas such as, "He wants you to call him tonight" or "She would buy it if she could," except in the way just stated? Our explanation of the Portuguese subjunctive will include these situations and some others where the use of the subjunctive is unavoidable.

Formation of the Subjunctive Tenses; Present Subjunctive

We first came upon the subjunctive, without knowing it, when we learned the polite command forms (page 53), which are really part of the subjunctive (third person singular and plural). The present subjunctive of almost all verbs is formed by taking the first person singular of the present indicative (the normal present tense, pages 50–51), dropping the *-o*, and adding, for *-ar* verbs, *-e, -es, -e, -emos, -eis, -em*; for *-er* and *-ir* verbs, *-a, -as, -a, -amos, -ais, -am*.

INFIN.	1ST PERS. SING. PRES. INDIC.	PRESENT SUBJUNCTIVE
falar (to speak)	fal*o*	fale, fales, fale, falemos, faleis, falem
vender (to sell)	vend*o*	venda, vendas, venda, vendamos, vendais, vendam
partir (to depart)	part*o*	parta, partas, parta, partamos, partais, partam

For the present subjunctive of irregular verbs see Appendix D. Appendixes B and C give further details for certain types of regular verbs.

Imperfect Subjunctive

All Portuguese verbs without exception form the imperfect subjunctive (the most widely used past tense of the subjunctive) by dropping the ending -*ram* of the third person plural of the past definite (indicative) and adding the endings -*sse*, -*sses*, -*sse*, -*ssemos*, -*sseis*, -*ssem*:

INFIN.	3RD PERS. PL. OF PAST DEFINITE	IMPERFECT SUBJUNCTIVE
falar (to speak)	fala*ram*	falasse, falasses, falasse, falássemos, falásseis, falassem
vender (to sell)	vende*ram*	vendesse, vendesses, vendesse, vendêssemos, vendêsseis, vendessem
partir (to depart)	parti*ram*	partisse, partisses, partisse, partíssemos, partísseis, partissem

For the *present perfect subjunctive* see the full paradigm of regular verbs in Appendix A.

Past Perfect Subjunctive

This tense is important chiefly for certain types of if-sentences (see page 67). You form it by placing the imperfect subjunctive of the helping verb *ter* (less frequently *haver*) before the past participle of the main verb:

INFIN.	PAST PERFECT SUBJUNCTIVE
falar (to speak)	tivesse falado, tivesses falado, tivesse falado, tivéssemos falado, tivésseis falado, tivessem falado
escrever (to write)	tivesse escrito, tivesses escrito, tivesse escrito, tivéssemos escrito, tivésseis escrito, tivessem escrito

Future Subjunctive

In the other popular Romance languages this tense is now archaic or non-existent, but it is still very much alive in Portuguese. It is formed by dropping the ending -*ram* from the third person plural of the past definite (indicative) and adding the endings -*r*, -*res*, -*r*, -*rmos*, -*rdes*, -*rem*:

INFIN.	3RD PERS. PL. OF PAST DEFINITE	FUTURE SUBJUNCTIVE
falar (to speak)	fala*ram*	falar, falares, falar, falarmos, falardes, falarem
vender (to sell)	vende*ram*	vender, venderes, vender, vendermos, venderdes, venderem
partir (to depart)	parti*ram*	partir, partires, partir, partirmos, partirdes, partirem

For the *future perfect subjunctive* see Appendix A.

Uses of the Subjunctive

The main uses of the subjunctive are as follows:

THE PRESENT SUBJUNCTIVE AND THE PAST TENSES OF THE SUBJUNCTIVE

1. After a verb of desiring, requesting, permitting, forbidding, etc., in the main clause of a sentence, the subjunctive is used in the dependent clause when the dependent clause has a *different* subject.

Desejo que ela *esteja* lá a horas. (pres. subj.)
[I want that she *be* there on time.]
I want her to be there on time.

Desejava que ela *estivesse* lá a horas. (imperf. subj.)
I wanted her to be there on time.

But compare:

Desejo (Desejava) *estar* lá a horas. (infin.)
I want (I wanted) *to be* there on time [that is, myself].

2. After expressions of emotion, such as hoping, fearing, being glad, being sorry, etc., when there is a change of subject.

Espero que eles *cheguem* hoje. (pres. subj.)
I hope that they *arrive* (OR *will arrive*) today.

Lamentei que eles *chegassem*. (imperf. subj.)
I was sorry that they *arrived*.

Receava que ele já *tivesse vindo*. (past perf. subj.)
I was afraid that he *had* already *come*.

3. After verbs of doubting:

Duvido que *falem* português. (pres. subj.)
I doubt that *they speak* Portuguese.

Duvidam que alguem *estivesse* lá. (imperf. subj.)
They doubt that anyone *was* there.

4. After many impersonal expressions, such as "it is necessary," "it is important," "it is possible," etc.*

É necessário que o Sr. *venha* cá esta noite. (pres. subj.)
It is necessary that you *come* here tonight.

É possível que ele agora *fale* inglês. (pres. subj.)
It is possible that he *speaks* English now.

5. After certain conjunctions, such as *antes que* (before), *logo que* (as soon as), *assim que* (as soon as), *posto que* (even if, although), *para que* (in order that), *a menos que* (unless), etc.

Assim que a *veja*, eu lhe direi isso. (pres. subj.)
As soon as *I see* her, I shall tell her that.

Posto que *fosse* verdade, quem creria isso? (imperf. subj.)
Even if *it were* true, who would believe that?

Generally, if the verb in the main clause is in the present, future or command form, the subjunctive verb will be in the present or imperfect; if the main verb is in the past or conditional, the subjunctive will be imperfect or past perfect. A closer study of the sample sentences we have given should settle many of your questions on the tenses used and the situations in English that they correspond to. The use of the imperfect and past perfect subjunctive in if-sentences will be discussed on page 67.

FUTURE SUBJUNCTIVE

Aside from its use in if-sentences (see page 67) and a few specialized uses, the future subjunctive is chiefly employed to express future time

---

* But not after *é certo* (it is certain), for example, because expressions of certainty do not call for the subjunctive.

after certain conjunctions, such as *quando* (when), *depois que* (after), etc.

Quando ele *vier* eu estarei aqui.
When he *comes* I shall be here.

The Subjunctive in If-Sentences

Study the following rules:

1. When the if-clause of an if-sentence (conditional sentence) implies an actual fact, the verb of the if-clause is in the indicative:

Se *tem* dinheiro, faça uma viagem!
If you *have* money, take a trip!

(implies that there is a good chance that you do have the money)

2. When the sentence is "contrary to fact" (that is, when the if's cannot be fulfilled), the imperfect subjunctive is generally used in the if-clause and the conditional (or sometimes the imperfect indicative) in the main clause when the *present* situation is being referred to:

Se eu *tivesse* dinheiro, *faria* (or *fazia*) uma viagem.
If I *had* money, *I would take* a trip.

(implies that I do not have the money *now*)

3. When, in a "contrary to fact" if-sentence, a *past* situation (what might have been) is being referred to, the past perfect subjunctive is used in the if-clause and the conditional perfect (or sometimes the pluperfect indicative) in the main clause:

Se eu *tivesse tido* dinheiro, *teria feito* (or *tinha feito*) uma viagem.
If I *had had* money, *I would have taken* a trip.

(implies that I did not have the money *then*)

4. When the if-clause refers to a future situation, the future subjunctive is used in the if-clause:

Se eu *tiver* dinheiro, *farei* uma viagem.
If I *have* money, *I shall take* a trip.

(implies that I hope to have the money in the future)

Reflexive Verbs

Comparison of Reflexive Verbs in English and Portuguese

In English, we say: "I get up," "I wash," "I shave," "I dress." In each case the action of the verb refers back to the subject. We might also say: "I wash myself," "I shave myself," "I dress myself." This is what is done in Portuguese, where the reflexive pronoun (*me, te, se, nos, vos, se*) must be used with all reflexive verbs. The position of these pronouns with regard to the verb is exactly the same as for the object pronouns discussed previously (see pages 36 and 60).

The Present (Indicative) Tense of Reflexive Verbs

deitar-se (to lie down, go to bed)

deito-me	OR eu me deito	I lie down
deitas-te	OR tu te deitas	you (fam. sing.) lie down
deita-se	OR ele (ela; o Sr.) se deita	he (she, it) lies down; you (polite sing.) lie down
deitamo-nos	OR nós nos deitamos	we lie down
deitais-vos	OR vós vos deitais	you (formal fam. pl.) lie down
deitam-se	OR eles (elas; os Srs.) se deitam	they lie down; you (polite pl.) lie down

Note that the -*s* of the we-form of the verb is dropped when the reflexive pronoun *nos* follows it.

Other Tenses of Reflexive Verbs

PAST DEFINITE

deitei-me	OR eu me deitei	I lay down

IMPERFECT

deitava-me	OR eu me deitava	I was lying down

PLUPERFECT

tinha-me deitado	OR eu me tinha deitado	I had lain down

FUTURE

deitar-me-ei	OR eu me deitarei	I shall lie down

CONDITIONAL

deitar-me-ia	OR eu me deitaria	I would lie down

POLITE IMPERATIVE SING.

deite-se	lie down

Important Reflexive Verbs

Reflexive verbs are more frequent in Portuguese than in English. Like *deitar-se*, so also the verbs *levantar-se* (to get up), *sentar-se* (to sit down) and *vestir-se* (to get dressed), for instance, are reflexive in Portuguese while they are not in English.

acordar-se	to wake up
despedir-se	to say goodbye, take one's leave
divertir-se	to have a good time
esposar-se	to get married
esquecer-se	to forget
sentir-se bem (mal)	to feel well (ill)
zangar-se	to get angry

Uses of the Reflexive

The following sentences illustrate reflexive and non-reflexive uses of verbs. Study them carefully.

Levanto o peso.	*I raise* the weight.
Levanto-me cedo.	*I get up* early.
Ele *chamou* os bombeiros.	He *called* the firemen.
Ele *chama-se* Jorge.	He *is called* George (OR His name
[He calls himself George.]	is George).
Não *vista* essa camisa.	Don't *put on* that shirt.
Nunca *me visto* de preto.	*I* never *dress* in black.
Eu *lavo* as mãos.	I *wash* my hands.
[I wash the hands.]	
Eu *lavo-me* todos os dias.	I *wash* (OR take a bath) every day.

The reflexive is also used to express the idea of "each other" or "one another." This meaning is sometimes made clearer or more emphatic by adding *um ao outro* (one to the other), *uns aos outros*, etc. (varying with the number and gender involved).

Nós *nos encontrámos* no restaurante.	We *met each other* in the restaurant.
Eles *amam-se um ao outro.*	They *love each other.*

In Portuguese, the reflexive is also often used where English uses an impersonal construction such as "Here one speaks English," or "They say it is so," or "We do it that way," or where in English the passive would be used: "This is how it is said."

Aqui *fala-se* português.   Portuguese *is spoken* here.

Diz-se que ele é muito rico.   *They say* that he is very rich.

Come-se bem neste restaurante.   *One dines* well (OR The food is
                                   good) in this restaurant.

The Passive Voice

In Portuguese, the passive is formed as it is in English, by using
the verb "to be" (*ser* is the verb used in this case) with the past
participle: "The house *was bought* by Mrs. Green." The past
participle is used like an adjective here and must agree with the
subject in number and gender.* The reflexive construction, discussed above, is often used instead of the passive in Portuguese.†
However, when the person doing the action is mentioned, it is
impossible to use the reflexive and the passive must be used.

A casa *foi vendida* por   The house *was sold* by my uncle.
   meu tio.
(COMPARE: Aqui *vendem-se*
   livros.   Books *are sold* here.)
Os rapazes *serão punidos*.   The boys *will be* punished.

Prepositions and Infinitives

Verbs Followed Directly by the Infinitive

As in English ("I must leave now"), many common Portuguese
verbs are followed directly by the infinitive without an intervening
preposition.   Study these examples:

Não quero ir ao teatro.   I do not want to go to the theater.
Ela prefere ficar connosco. She prefers to stay with us.
Que devemos fazer agora?   What should we do now?
Sabe o Sr. cozer?   Do you know how to cook?
Nunca pude fazer isso.   I was never able to do that.

As is apparent from the last example, there are many cases where
in English you will find the infinitive preceded by "to" while no
preposition is used in Portuguese.

* When a verb has two past participles, the irregular form is used in the passive
voice (see Appendix D for irregular forms).

† The reflexive construction is generally used only when the subject is inanimate:
"*It* is said," "*Books* are sold here," etc.

Verbs Followed by *a* or *de* before the Infinitive

Study the following sentences:

Aprendemos a ler e escrever.	We are learning to read and write.
Ensina-me a nadar.	He is teaching me to swim.
Começo a falar espanhol.	I am beginning to speak Spanish.
Ajude-me a fechar a janela.	Help me to close the window.
Gosta o Sr. de viajar?	Do you like to travel?
Esqueci-me de pôr no correio a carta.	I forgot to mail the letter.
Tratam de chamar um táxi.	They are trying to call a cab.

Only repeated use will help you to remember which verbs are followed by *a*, which by *de*, and which take no preposition at all. (*Em*, *por* and other prepositions also occur between verbs and infinitives). The beginner will do well, however, to remember the examples given.

The Present Participle and the Infinitive

In English, the present participle is used after prepositions (before *leaving*, after *eating*, without *thinking*). In Portuguese, it is never so used, but the infinitive is used instead.

antes de *partir*	before *leaving*
depois de *comer*	after *eating*
sem *pensar*	without *thinking*
ao *entrar*	upon *entering*

Antes de partir fechei todas as janelas.	*Before leaving* I closed all the windows.
Não é bom banhar-se logo *depois de comer*.	It is not good to bathe immediately *after eating*.
Fala sempre *sem pensar*.	He always speaks *without thinking*.
Ao entrar no hotel encontrei os meus amigos de São Paulo.	*Upon entering* the hotel I met my friends from São Paulo.

The Personal Infinitive

You will notice that in each of the sentences just given, the implied subject of the Portuguese infinitive is the same as the main subject of the sentence; i.e., the sense is "*I* closed the windows before *my* leaving," "*I* met my friends upon *my* entering the hotel," etc. The situation is slightly different if we want to use the Portuguese preposition-plus-infinitive construction to express the meaning: "*I* closed the windows before *their* arriving" or "Upon *our* entering the hotel *I* met my friends," i.e., when the subject changes. Portuguese has a form unique among all languages for handling just this situation: the personal infinitive. This is merely the infinitive you have already learned, with personal endings added (except in the first and third persons singular):

falar (to speak)

(eu) falar	(nós) falarmos
(tu) falares	(vós) falardes
(ele) falar	(eles) falarem

These endings are the same as those of the future subjunctive and, in fact, the personal infinitive looks exactly like the future subjunctive for all regular verbs. Even if you do not use the personal infinitive yourself, you should be able to recognize it. The following sentences illustrate its principal uses:

Eu falarei com eles antes de *partirem*.	I shall speak with them before *they leave*.

Compare:

Eu falarei com eles antes de *partir*.	I shall speak with them before *leaving* (i.e., before *I* leave).
Ao entrarmos no hotel encontrei os meus amigos.	*As we entered* the hotel I met my friends.
É bom *estudarem*.	It is good *for them to study*.
Esta lição é *para eu aprender*.	This lesson is *for me to study*.

Note in the last sentence that a subject pronoun can be used with this personal infinitive. The personal infinitive construction may also be used for greater clarity even when the subject of the infinitive is the same as the main subject of the sentence.

The personal infinitive construction can generally be avoided by using a clause instead:

Os rapazes partiram depressa *por terem visto** o pai.
Os rapazes partiram depressa *porque viram* o pai.
The boys left quickly *because they saw* their father.

---

* In this sentence, *ter visto* is a past infinitive formed with the infinitive of the helping verb *ter* and the past participle. The personal endings are added to the *ter*. A literal rendering of *por terem visto* would be "because-of their-having seen."

É preciso *fazermos* isso.
É preciso *que façamos* isso.
It is necessary *for us to do* (or *that we do*) that.

Idiomatic Constructions

We have seen that there are many parallel constructions in English and Portuguese. But there are also many idiomatic expressions in Portuguese which have no exact parallel in English. These cannot be translated literally, nor can they always be explained grammatically or logically. It is important to learn most of these expressions because without them you would be unable to say many of the common things you are most anxious to say.

The Verb *Fazer*

Fazer (to do, to make) is used in a variety of idiomatic expressions where English uses other verbs.

1. Expressions of weather:

Faz bom (mau) tempo.	The weather is good (bad). [It *makes* good (bad) weather.]
Faz frio. *Faz* vento?	It is cold. Is it windy?
Faz sol e *faz* calor.	It is sunny and it is hot.

2. Other idiomatic uses:

fazer perguntas	to ask questions
fazer compras	to shop, go shopping
fazer uma visita	to pay a call
fazer uma viagem	to take a trip
fazer um passeio	to take a walk, to go for a ride
fazer a barba	to shave
fazer falta	to be needed, to be lacking
Faz-se tarde.	It is getting late.
Não *faz* mal.	It's all right, it doesn't matter.
Faz uma semana que cheguei.	I arrived a week ago. [*It makes* a week that I arrived.]

The Verb *Ter*

"To be hungry, thirsty, warm, etc." are rendered in Portuguese by the verb *ter* with the noun: "to have hunger, thirst, etc."

Tenho fome.	I am hungry.
Temos sede.	We are thirsty.
Tem calor?	Are you warm?
Têm frio.	They are cold.
Tenho sono.	I am sleepy.
Temos medo.*	We are afraid.
Tenho muita pressa.	I am in a great hurry.
Tem razão.	He is right.
Tenho vergonha.	I am ashamed.

Observe also:

Tenho vinte anos.	I am twenty years old. [*I have* twenty years.]
Tenho que sair.	I must go out.
Tenha cuidado!	Be careful!
Que é que o Sr. *tem?*	What is the matter with you?
Não *tenho* nada.	Nothing is the matter with me.
Tenha a bondade de vir.	Please come. [*Have* the goodness to come.]
Não *tem*† muita gente no teatro.	There aren't many people in the theater. [*It has* not many people in the theater.]

The Verb *Haver*

The uses of this verb are limited today. It is very infrequently used as the helping verb in compound tenses (*ter* is much more common) and some of its principal idiomatic uses are being taken over by other verbs. Study the following idioms:

Há vinte estudantes na classe.	There are twenty students in the class. [*It has* twenty students in the class.]
Há três anos que estudo francês. (also frequently: *Faz* três anos que estudo francês.)	I have been studying French for three years. [*It has* three years that I study French.]

* The first six items in the list of *ter* idioms can also be expressed in Portuguese as "I am with hunger, thirst, etc.": *Estou com* fome; *estamos com* sede; *está com* calor?; *estão com* frio; *estou com* sono; *estamos com* medo.

† In conversational Portuguese, *tem* is sometimes used instead of *há* in the meaning "there is, there are." See idioms with *haver*.

Há um mês que cheguei.	I arrived a month ago. [*It has* a
(also frequently:	month that I arrived.]
Faz um mês que cheguei.)	
Hei-de ir ao teatro.	*I shall* go to the theater.
(OR:	
Tenho que ir ao teatro.)	

The Verbs *Ser* and *Estar*

Although *ser* and *estar* both mean "to be," they are not inter-changeable. In general, *ser* expresses an inherent or permanent quality of "being," while *estar* denotes a temporary location or temporary characteristic. Study the following sentences carefully:

estar (TEMPORARY)	*ser* (PERMANENT)
Eu *estou* aqui.	Eu *sou* americano.
(I *am* here, or I *am standing* here.)	I *am* an American.
A água *está* fria.	A água *é* transparente.
The water *is* cold.	Water *is* transparent.
Ela *está* pálida.	Ela *é* pálida.
She *is* pale. (She has just turned pale or she is pale from a temporary illness.)	She *is* pale. (Her complexion is naturally pale.)
O livro *está* sobre a mesa.	Londres *é* em Inglaterra.
The book *is* on the table.	London *is* in England.

The verb *ser* is used in expressions of possession, origin and time, in impersonal phrases and in the passive voice:

O livro *é* meu.	The book *is* mine.
Ela *é* do Rio.	She *is* from Rio.
São dez horas.	It is ten o'clock. [*They are* ten hours.]
É impossível.	*It is* impossible.
A carta *foi* escrita por mim.	The letter *was* written by me.

The verb *estar* is used in the progressive construction (which describes what someone is doing *at the moment*):

Estou escrevendo uma carta.	*I am* writing a letter.

The Verbs *Saber* and *Conhecer*

Although both *saber* and *conhecer* are translated by "to know," they are not interchangeable. Essentially, *saber* means "to know" in the sense of "to have knowledge"; *conhecer*, in the sense of "to be acquainted with." *Conhecer* may also be used in the sense of "to meet," "to make the acquaintance of."

Ele *sabe* de cor o poema todo.	He *knows* the whole poem by heart.
Eu *sei* onde está o livro.	I *know* where the book is.
Sabemos nadar.	*We know how* to swim.
Conheço esse homem.	*I know* that man.
Gostaria de *conhecê*-la.	I would like to *meet* her.
Conhece aquele restaurante?	*Are you acquainted with* that restaurant?

The Verbs *Ir* and *Andar*

Some idioms with *ir* (to go):

Como *vai* o Sr.?	How *are* you?
Eu *vou* melhor.	I *am feeling* better.

Some idioms with *andar* (to walk, move, go around):

O relógio não *anda*.	The watch has stopped (i.e., *does* not *go*).
O carro não *anda*.	The car *does* not *go*.
Ontem *andei a cavalo*.	Yesterday *I went horseback riding*.

Idioms with *Acabar, Dar, Ficar, Levar, Mandar, Passar* and *Querer*

With *acabar* (to finish):

Ele *acaba de* chegar.	He *has just* arrived.
Eu *acabo de* ler o livro.	I *have just finished* reading the book.

With *dar* (to give):

A janela *dá para* o mar.	The window *faces* the sea.
Ela *dá para* música.	She *shows talent in* music.
Eu *dei com* João na rua.	I *met* John in the street.
Ele *dá-se bem com* Maria.	He *gets along well with* Mary.
Eu *dou-me mal* neste clima.	This climate disagrees with me. [*I give myself badly* in this climate.]

With *ficar* (to remain):

Este chapéu *fica*-lhe *bem*.	This hat *is becoming to* her.

With *levar* (to carry):

Quanto tempo *leva* o avião daqui a Washington?	How long *does* the plane *take* from here to Washington?

With *mandar* (to order):

Mandei fazer um vestido.	*I had* a dress *made* (to order).
Mande chamar o médico.	Send for the doctor. [*Have* the doctor *called*.]

With *passar* (to pass):

Como *passa* o Sr.? *Passo* bem.	How *are* you *doing*? I *feel* fine.
A criada *passou a ferro* o lenço.	The maid *ironed* the handkerchief.

With *querer* (to want):

Que *quer dizer* essa palavra?	What *does* that word *mean*?
Maria *quer* muito *a* João.	Mary *is* very *fond of* John.
Queira fechar a porta, *por favor*.	*Please* close the door.

SOME USEFUL EXPRESSIONS

Study these useful expressions which have not appeared in the body of this book:

Que horas são?	What time is it? [What hours are?]
São oito e meia.	It is half past eight.
É meio-dia.	It is noon.
Sinto a falta dos meus.	I miss my family.
Não importa.	It doesn't matter.
Que pena!	Too bad! What a pity!
Bom dia.	Good morning. Good day.
Boa tarde.	Good afternoon. (Also, "Good evening" for early in the evening.)
Boa noite.	Good night. (Also, "Good evening" for later in the evening.)
Até logo.	So long.
Até amanhã.	See you tomorrow.
De tarde.	In the afternoon.
Depois de amanhã.	The day after tomorrow.
Antes de ontem.	The day before yesterday.
Daqui a pouco.	In a little while.
Há pouco.	A little while ago.
Por fim.	Finally. At last.
Outra vez.	Again.
Em vez de.	Instead of.
Talvez.	Perhaps.
Assim.	Therefore. Thus.
Ao menos.	At least.
Naturalmente.	Of course.
Como não!	Naturally!
Todo o mundo.	Everybody.
Toda a gente.	Everybody.
Tudo.	Everything.
Com todo o gosto.	Willingly. With pleasure.

78

Muito obrigado (obrigada).	Many thanks. [Much obliged—agrees with gender of speaker.]
Não tem de quê.	You're welcome.
Desculpe-me.	Excuse me.
Sem dúvida.	Without doubt. No doubt.

Appendix A

COMPLETE PARADIGM OF
THE THREE REGULAR CONJUGATIONS

For the convenience of the beginner and the tourist we presented in the body of the book only those tenses of the regular verbs that are most commonly used. For the sake of completeness and as a handy reference for the student we will now show the full conjugation of every tense, explaining the formation of those tenses that have not been presented earlier.

FIRST CONJUGATION	SECOND CONJUGATION	THIRD CONJUGATION

INFINITIVE

falar	vender	partir

TENSES OF THE INDICATIVE

PRESENT

falo	vendo	parto
falas	vendes	partes
fala	vende	parte
falamos	vendemos	partimos
falais	vendeis	partis
falam	vendem	partem

IMPERFECT

falava	vendia	partia
falavas	vendias	partias
falava	vendia	partia
falávamos	vendíamos	partíamos
faláveis	vendíeis	partíeis
falavam	vendiam	partiam

FIRST CONJUGATION	SECOND CONJUGATION	THIRD CONJUGATION

PAST DEFINITE (PRETERIT)

falei	vendi	parti
falaste	vendeste	partiste
falou	vendeu	partiu
falámos	vendemos	partimos
falastes	vendestes	partistes
falaram	venderam	partiram

PRESENT PERFECT (explained below)

tenho falado	tenho vendido	tenho partido
tens falado	tens vendido	tens partido
tem falado	tem vendido	tem partido
temos falado	temos vendido	temos partido
tendes falado	tendes vendido	tendes partido
têm falado	têm vendido	têm partido

PLUPERFECT (COMPOUND TYPE)

tinha falado	tinha vendido	tinha partido
tinhas falado	tinhas vendido	tinhas partido
tinha falado	tinha vendido	tinha partido
tínhamos falado	tínhamos vendido	tínhamos partido
tínheis falado	tínheis vendido	tínheis partido
tinham falado	tinham vendido	tinham partido

SECONDARY PLUPERFECT (explained below)

falara	vendera	partira
falaras	venderas	partiras
falara	vendera	partira
faláramos	vendêramos	partíramos
faláreis	vendêreis	partíreis
falaram	venderam	partiram

FUTURE

falarei	venderei	partirei
falarás	venderás	partirás
falará	venderá	partirá
falaremos	venderemos	partiremos
falareis	vendereis	partireis
falarão	venderão	partirão

FIRST CONJUGATION	SECOND CONJUGATION	THIRD CONJUGATION
FUTURE PERFECT (explained below)		
terei falado	terei vendido	terei partido
terás falado	terás vendido	terás partido
terá falado	terá vendido	terá partido
teremos falado	teremos vendido	teremos partido
tereis falado	tereis vendido	tereis partido
terão falado	terão vendido	terão partido
CONDITIONAL		
falaria	venderia	partiria
falarias	venderias	partirias
falaria	venderia	partiria
falaríamos	venderíamos	partiríamos
falaríeis	venderíeis	partiríeis
falariam	venderiam	partiriam
CONDITIONAL PERFECT (explained below)		
teria falado	teria vendido	teria partido
terias falado	terias vendido	terias partido
teria falado	teria vendido	teria partido
teríamos falado	teríamos vendido	teríamos partido
teríeis falado	teríeis vendido	teríeis partido
teriam falado	teriam vendido	teriam partido

TENSES OF THE SUBJUNCTIVE

FIRST	SECOND	THIRD
PRESENT		
fale	venda	parta
fales	vendas	partas
fale	venda	parta
falemos	vendamos	partamos
faleis	vendais	partais
falem	vendam	partam
IMPERFECT		
falasse	vendesse	partisse
falasses	vendesses	partisses
falasse	vendesse	partisse
falássemos	vendêssemos	partíssemos
falásseis	vendêsseis	partísseis
falassem	vendessem	partissem

FIRST CONJUGATION	SECOND CONJUGATION	THIRD CONJUGATION

PRESENT PERFECT (explained below)

tenha falado	tenha vendido	tenha partido
tenhas falado	tenhas vendido	tenhas partido
tenha falado	tenha vendido	tenha partido
tenhamos falado	tenhamos vendido	tenhamos partido
tenhais falado	tenhais vendido	tenhais partido
tenham falado	tenham vendido	tenham partido

PAST PERFECT

tivesse falado	tivesse vendido	tivesse partido
tivesses falado	tivesses vendido	tivesses partido
tivesse falado	tivesse vendido	tivesse partido
tivéssemos falado	tivéssemos vendido	tivéssemos partido
tivésseis falado	tivésseis vendido	tivésseis partido
tivessem falado	tivessem vendido	tivessem partido

FUTURE

falar	vender	partir
falares	venderes	partires
falar	vender	partir
falarmos	vendermos	partirmos
falardes	venderdes	partirdes
falarem	venderem	partirem

FUTURE PERFECT (explained below)

tiver falado	tiver vendido	tiver partido
tiveres falado	tiveres vendido	tiveres partido
tiver falado	tiver vendido	tiver partido
tivermos falado	tivermos vendido	tivermos partido
tiverdes falado	tiverdes vendido	tiverdes partido
tiverem falado	tiverem vendido	tiverem partido

OTHER FORMS

PRESENT PARTICIPLE

falando	vendendo	partindo

PAST PARTICIPLE

falado	vendido	partido

FIRST CONJUGATION	SECOND CONJUGATION	THIRD CONJUGATION

PERSONAL INFINITIVE

falar	vender	partir
falares	venderes	partires
falar	vender	partir
falarmos	vendermos	partirmos
falardes	venderdes	partirdes
falarem	venderem	partirem

IMPERATIVE (COMMAND FORM)

(tu)	fala	vende	parte
(o Sr.)	fale	venda	parta
(nós)	falemos OR	vendamos OR	partamos OR
	vamos falar	vamos vender	vamos partir
(vós)	falai	vendei	parti
(os Srs.)	falem	vendam	partam

The Present Perfect Tense (Indicative)

The Portuguese present perfect tense corresponds in meaning with the same tense in English ("I have come," "I have told"), but its use is much more limited in Portuguese, where the past definite (or preterit) tense is used more often for this purpose. In general, Portuguese employs the present perfect tense only when an action which has started in the past is considered as extending into the present: for instance, "It has been very cold this winter [and it still is]" or "I have been studying since three o'clock." The present perfect tense is formed with the present tense of the helping verb *ter* (or sometimes *haver*) and the past participle.

Tem feito muito frio este inverno.
[It has made very cold this winter.]
It has been very cold this winter.

Tenho estudado desde as três horas.
[I have studied since the three hours.]
I have been studying since three o'clock.

The Secondary Pluperfect Tense

This type of pluperfect is not compound; it has its own set of endings and uses no helping verb. The secondary pluperfect is almost never used in conversation, but you are likely to come across it in literature. All verbs without exception form this tense in the same way: the ending *-ram* is dropped from the third person plural form of the *past definite* tense, and the endings *-ra*, *-ras*, *-ra*, *-ramos*, *-reis*, *-ram* are added. This type of pluperfect has exactly the same meaning (I had spoken, sold, etc.) as the more conversational compound type.

Quando cheguei ele já *tinha falado*. (conversational)
Quando cheguei ele já *falara*. (literary)
When I arrived he *had* already *spoken*.

Tinha-lhe *escrito* antes de partir.. (conversational)
Escrevera-lhe antes de partir. (literary)
I had written to him before leaving.

The Future Perfect Tense (Indicative)

The future perfect tense is formed with the future tense of the helping verb *ter* (less frequently, *haver*) and the past participle. This tense is used to refer to an action that *will have* taken place before another action in the future.

Ela *terá feito* isso antes de domingo.
She *will have done* that before Sunday.

The Conditional Perfect Tense

The conditional perfect is formed with the conditional of the helping verb *ter* (less frequently, *haver*) and the past participle. It is used like the corresponding tense in English.

Eu o *teria feito* com prazer.
I *would have done* it with pleasure.

The Present Perfect Subjunctive

The use of this tense of the subjunctive is as restricted as that of he present perfect indicative (see above). It is formed with the present subjunctive of the helping verb *ter* (less frequently, *haver*) and the past participle.

Lamento que ele já *tenha vindo*.
I am sorry that he *has* already *come*.

The Future Perfect Subjunctive

This rarely used tense is formed with the future subjunctive of the helping verb *ter* (less frequently, *haver*) plus the past participle.

Appendix B

ORTHOGRAPHIC-CHANGING VERBS

The verbs considered in this appendix are mostly perfectly regular, but the final consonant of their stem undergoes certain predictable *spelling* changes designed to show that its pronunciation is preserved under all circumstances.* The *stem* of a verb is what remains after the infinitive ending -*ar*, -*er* or -*ir* is dropped; thus, *fal-* is the stem of *falar*, *vend-* is the stem of *vender*, etc.)

The following table shows (a) the consonant changes needed before certain vowels, (b) the inflectional endings in the various tenses that are involved† and (c) examples.

---

* For example, Portuguese *c*, like English *c*, is "hard" before *a, o* and *u*, "soft" before *e* and *i*. In *all* forms of a verb like *marcar* (to mark) the *c* has its hard sound; when the inflectional ending begins with an *e* (as in the first person singular of the past definite), you can no longer write *marcei*, but must write *marquei* (*qu* signifies a "*k*"-sound before *e* and *i*) to show that the hard sound is retained.

† Inflectional endings not shown in the table are not involved.

Table of Orthographic Changes in Verbs

	CHANGES			FORMS AFFECTED				EXAMPLES		
IF INFIN. ENDS IN	CHANGE	TO	BEFORE	PRES. IND.	PAST DEF.	PRES. SUBJ.	POLITE IMPER.	INFIN.	SAME AS INFIN.	NEEDS CHANGE
-car	c	qu	e	—	-quei	-que, -ques, -que, -quemos, -queis, -quem	-que, -quem	marcar (to mark)	marco (I mark)	marquei (I marked)
-gar	g	gu	e	—	-guei	-gue, -gues, -gue, -guemos, -gueis, -guem	-gue, -guem	chegar (to arrive)	chega (he arrives)	chegue (arrive!)
-çar	ç	c	e	—	-cei	-ce, -ces, -ce, -cemos, -ceis, -cem	-ce, -cem	começar (to begin)	começam (they begin)	comecei (I began)
-cer	c	ç	o, a	-ço	—	-ça, -ças, -ça, -çamos, -çais, -çam	-ça, -çam	conhecer (to know)	conhece (he knows)	conheço (I know)
-ger	g	j	o, a	-jo	—	-ja, -jas, -ja, -jamos, -jais, -jam	-ja, -jam	eleger (to elect)	elegemos (we elect)	eleja (elect!)

-guer*	gu	g	o, a	-go	—	-ga, -gas, -ga, -gamos, -gais, -gam	-ga, -gam	*erguer* (to raise)	*ergue* (he raises)	*ergo* (I raise)
-gir	g	j	o, a	-jo	—	-ja, -jas, -ja, -jamos, -jais, -jam	-ja, -jam	*fugir* (to flee)	*fugimos* (we flee)	*fujo* (I flee)
-guir*	gu	g	o, a	-go	—	-ga, -gas, -ga, -gamos, -gais, -gam	-ga, -gam	*seguir* (to follow)	*seguimos* (we follow)	*siga* (follow!)

* This applies only to verbs in which the *u* is silent and merely a spelling convention to show that the *g* has the "hard" sound (as in the English word "*goat*").

Appendix C
RADICAL-CHANGING VERBS

The verbs considered in this appendix are regular, except that in certain situations the *vowel* of their stem* undergoes certain predictable changes. Only the present tense of the indicative and subjunctive and the polite command forms are affected.

1. First conjugation verbs with infinitives ending in -*ear* change the stem vowel *e* to *ei* throughout the singular and in the third person plural. The verbs *recear* (to fear) and *cear* (to eat supper) are thus conjugated as follows in the tenses involved:

PRES. IND.	PRES. SUBJ.	POLITE COMMAND FORMS
receio	receie	receie
receias	receies	receiem
receia	receie	
receamos	receemos	
receais	receeis	
receiam	receiem	

2. Several important third conjugation verbs with the stem vowels *e* or *o* change the *e* to *i* and the *o* to *u* in the first person singular of the present indicative and throughout the present subjunctive (as well as the polite command forms). Thus *preferir* (to prefer) and *dormir* (to sleep) give:

PRES. IND.		PRES. SUBJ.		POLITE COMMAND FORMS
prefiro	durmo	prefira	durma	
preferes	dormes	prefiras	durmas	prefira, prefiram
prefere	dorme	prefira	durma	
preferimos	dormimos	prefiramos	durmamos	durma, durmam
preferis	dormis	prefirais	durmais	
preferem	dormem	prefiram	durmam	

* See Appendix B for an explanation of "stem."

Conjugated like *preferir* are: *mentir* (to tell a lie), *repetir* (to repeat), *seguir* (to follow), *sentir* (to feel, to be sorry), *servir* (to serve) and *vestir-se* (to get dressed). *Cobrir* (to cover) is conjugated like *dormir*.

3. A few important third conjugation verbs with the stem vowel *u* change the *u* to *o* in the second and third persons of the singular and the third person plural of the present indicative only. Thus *subir* (to ascend, climb) gives:

PRES. IND.: subo, sobes, sobe, subimos, subis, sobem

Conjugated like *subir* are: *consumir* (to consume), *fugir* (to flee), *sacudir* (to shake) and *sumir* (to sink).

Appendix D

IRREGULAR VERBS

The verbs considered in this appendix are conjugated irregularly in various tenses, or have irregular past participles. Note that once you know the past participle of any verb, you can form its compound tenses (present perfect indicative and subjunctive, compound type of pluperfect, past perfect subjunctive, future perfect indicative and subjunctive, and conditional perfect) perfectly regularly with the proper tenses of the helping verb plus the past participle. Therefore, compound tenses will not be considered in this appendix.

1. The following verbs are irregular only in the first person singular of the present indicative and therefore throughout the present subjunctive and polite command forms:

INFIN.	1ST SING. PRES. IND.	PRES. SUBJ.	POLITE COMMAND FORMS
medir (to measure)	meço	meça, meças, meça, etc.	meça, meçam
ouvir (to hear)	ouço	ouça, ouças, ouça, etc.	ouça, ouçam
pedir (to ask)	peço	peça, peças, peça, etc.	peça, peçam
despedir-se (to say goodbye)	despeço-me	despeça-me, despeças-te, despeça-se, etc.	despeça-se, despeçam-se
perder (to lose)	perco	perca, percas, perca, etc.	perca, percam
valer (to be worth)	valho	valha, valhas, valha, etc.	valha, valham

2. Third conjugation verbs with infinitives ending in -*uzir* end in -*uz* in the third person singular of the present indicative:

conduzir (to lead)   conduz (he leads)
produzir (to produce)   produz (he produces)

3. Many verbs have irregular past participles. Some of the most common are:

abrir (to open)   aberto (opened)
cobrir (to cover)   coberto (covered)
escrever (to write)   escrito (written)
ganhar (to gain, earn)   ganho (gained, earned)*
gastar (to spend, waste)   gasto (spent, wasted)*
pagar (to pay)   pago (paid)*

Some important verbs have two past participles, one regular and one irregular:

acender (to light)   acendido, aceso (lighted)
atender (to heed, attend to)   atendido, atento (attended to)
entregar (to deliver, entrust)   entregado, entregue (delivered, entrusted)
nascer (to be born)   nascido, nato (born)

In these verbs the regular form of the participle is generally used to form compound tenses along with the helping verb *ter* (or *haver*). The irregular forms are used when the participle is employed as an adjective, especially in the passive voice (see p. 70).

4. Some of the most common and important verbs in the language are very irregular in many of their tenses. They are shown in the following table:†

---

* The regular past participle forms *ganhado*, *gastado* and *pagado* are now archaic.
† No compound tenses need to be shown. Furthermore, since *all* verbs form the secondary pluperfect (see p. 85), the imperfect subjunctive (see p. 64) and the future subjunctive (see p. 65) in the same way—by adding the appropriate endings to the basic form of the past definite—these tenses are not shown. Only four verbs are irregular in the imperfect indicative, and only three in the future indicative and conditional; these forms are shown separately after the table. The only irregular present participle is *pondo* (from *pôr*).

TABLE OF IRREGULAR VERBS

INFIN.	PAST PART.	PRES. IND.	PRES. SUBJ.	PAST DEF.	POLITE COMMAND FORMS
crer (to believe)	regular	creio crês crê cremos credes crêem	creia creias creia creiamos creiais creiam	cri crêste creu cremos crêstes creram	creia, creiam
dar (to give)	regular	dou dás dá damos dais dão	dê dês dê demos deis dêem	dei deste deu demos destes deram	dê, dêem
dizer (to say, tell)	dito	digo dizes diz dizemos dizeis dizem	diga digas diga digamos digais digam	disse disseste disse dissemos dissestes disseram	diga, digam
estar (to be)	regular	estou estás está estamos estais estão	esteja estejas esteja estejamos estejais estejam	estive estiveste esteve estivemos estivestes estiveram	esteja, estejam

fazer (to do, make)	feito	faço fazes faz fazemos fazeis fazem	faça faças faça façamos façais façam	fiz fizeste fêz fizemos fizestes fizeram	faça, façam
haver (to have)	regular	hei hás há havemos haveis hão	haja hajas haja hajamos hajais hajam	houve houveste houve houvemos houvestes houveram	haja, hajam
ir (to go)	regular	vou vais vai vamos ides vão	vá vás vá vamos vades vão	fui foste foi fomos fostes foram	vá, vão
poder (to be able)	regular	posso podes pode podemos podeis podem	possa possas possa possamos possais possam	pude podeste pôde pudemos pudestes puderam	possa, possam

TABLE OF IRREGULAR VERBS—(continued)

INFIN.	PAST PART.	PRES. IND.	PRES. SUBJ.	PAST DEF.	POLITE COMMAND FORMS
pôr* (to put, place)	posto	ponho pões põe pomos pondes põem	ponha ponhas ponha ponhamos ponhais ponham	pus puseste pôs pusemos pusestes puseram	ponha, ponham
querer (to want, be willing)	regular	quero queres quer queremos quereis querem	queira queiras queira queiramos queirais queiram	quis quiseste quis quisemos quisestes quiseram	queira, queiram
saber (to know)	regular	sei sabes sabe sabemos sabeis sabem	saiba saibas saiba saibamos saibais saibam	soube soubeste soube soubemos soubestes souberam	saiba, saibam
ser (to be)	regular	sou és é somos sois são	seja sejas seja sejamos sejais sejam	fui foste foi fomos fostes foram	seja, sejam

* *Pôr* is a contraction of an older infinitive form *poer* (second conjugation); *pôr* and its compounds are the only infinitives in modern Portuguese that do not end in -*ar*, -*er* or -*ir*.

	Past Participle	Present Indicative	Present Subjunctive	Preterite	Imperative
ter (to have)	regular	tenho tens tem temos tendes têm	tenha tenhas tenha tenhamos tenhais tenham	tive tiveste teve tivemos tivestes tiveram	tenha, tenham
trazer (to bring, wear, carry)	regular	trago trazes traz trazemos trazeis trazem	traga tragas traga tragamos tragais tragam	trouxe trouxeste trouxe trouxemos trouxestes trouxeram	traga, tragam
ver (to see)	visto	vejo vês vê vemos vêdes vêem	veja vejas veja vejamos vejais vejam	vi viste viu vimos vistes viram	veja, vejam
vir (to come)	vindo*	venho vens vem vimos vindes vêm	venha venhas venha venhamos venhais venham	vim vieste veio viemos viestes vieram	venha, venham

* Same as present participle.

Irregular Forms of the Imperfect Indicative

The verbs *pôr*, *ser*, *ter* and *vir* and their compounds are the only ones irregular in the imperfect indicative; they are conjugated as follows:

punha	era	tinha	vinha
punhas	eras	tinhas	vinhas
punha	era	tinha	vinha
púnhamos	éramos	tínhamos	vínhamos
púnheis	éreis	tínheis	vínheis
punham	eram	tinham	vinham

Irregular Forms of the Future Indicative and Conditional

The verbs *dizer*, *fazer* and *trazer* are the only ones irregular in the future indicative and conditional; they are conjugated as follows:

FUT. IND.			CONDIT.		
direi	farei	trarei	diria	faria	traria
dirás	farás	trarás	dirias	farias	trarias
dirá	fará	trará	diria	faria	traria
diremos	faremos	traremos	diríamos	faríamos	traríamos
direis	fareis	trareis	diríeis	faríeis	traríeis
dirão	farão	trarão	diriam	fariam	trariam

A GLOSSARY OF GRAMMATICAL TERMS

E. F. BLEILER

This section is intended to refresh your memory of grammatical terms or to clear up difficulties you may have had in understanding them. Before you work through the grammar, you should have a reasonably clear idea what the parts of speech and parts of a sentence are. This is not for reasons of pedantry, but simply because it is easier to talk about grammar if we agree upon terms. Grammatical terminology is as necessary to the study of grammar as the names of automobile parts are to garagemen.

This list is not exhaustive, and the definitions do not pretend to be complete, or to settle points of interpretation that grammarians have been disputing for the past several hundred years. It is a working analysis rather than a scholarly investigation. The definitions given, however, represent most typical American usage, and should serve for basic use.

The Parts of Speech

English words can be divided into eight important groups: nouns, adjectives, articles, verbs, adverbs, pronouns, prepositions, and conjunctions. The boundaries between one group of words and another are sometimes vague and ill-felt in English, but a good dictionary, like the *Webster Collegiate*, can help you make decisions in questionable cases. Always bear in mind, however, that the way a word is used in a sentence may be just as important as the nature of the word itself in deciding what part of speech the word is.

Nouns. *Nouns* are the *words* for *things* of all *sorts*, whether these *things* are real *objects* that you can see, or *ideas*, or *places*, or *qualities*, or *groups*, or more abstract *things*. *Examples* of *words* that are *nouns* are *cat, vase, door, shrub, wheat, university, mercy, intelligence, ocean, plumber, pleasure, society, army.* If you are in *doubt* whether a given *word* is a *noun*, try putting the *word* "my," or "this," or "large" (or some other *adjective*) in *front* of it. If it makes *sense* in the *sentence* the *chances* are that the *word* in *question* is a *noun*. [All the *words* in *italics* in this *paragraph* are *nouns*.]

Adjectives. Adjectives are the words which delimit or give you *specific* information about the *various* nouns in a sentence. They tell you size, color, weight, pleasantness, and many *other* qualities. *Such* words as *big, expensive, terrible, insipid, hot, delightful, ruddy, informative* are all *clear* adjectives. If you are in *any* doubt whether a *certain* word is an adjective, add -er to it, or put the word "more" or "too" in front of it. If it makes *good* sense in the sentence, and does not end in -ly, the chances are that it is an adjective. (Pronoun-adjectives will be described under pronouns.) [The adjectives in the *above* sentences are in italics.]

Articles. There are only two kinds of articles in English, and they are easy to remember. The definite article is "the" and the indefinite article is "a" or "an."

Verbs. Verbs *are* the words that *tell* what action, or condition, or relationship *is going* on. Such words as *was, is, jumps, achieved, keeps, buys, sells, has finished, run, will have, may, should pay, indicates* are all verb forms. *Observe* that a verb *can be composed* of more than one word, as *will have* and *should pay*, above; these *are called* compound verbs. As a rough guide for verbs, *try adding* -ed to the word you *are wondering* about, or *taking* off an -ed that *is* already there. If it *makes* sense, the chances *are* that it *is* a verb. (This *does* not always *work*, since the so-called strong or irregular verbs *make* forms by *changing* their middle vowels, like *spring, sprang, sprung*.) [Verbs in this paragraph *are* in italics.]

Adverbs. An adverb is a word that supplies additional information about a verb, an adjective, or another adverb. It *usually* indicates time, or manner, or place, or degree. It tells you *how*, or *when*, or *where*, or to what degree things are happening. Such words as *now, then, there, not, anywhere, never, somehow, always, very*, and most words ending in -ly are *ordinarily* adverbs. [Italicized words are adverbs.]

Pronouns. Pronouns are related to nouns, and take their place. (Some grammars and dictionaries group pronouns and nouns together as substantives.) *They* mention persons, or objects of any sort without actually giving their names.

There are several different kinds of pronouns. (1) Personal pronouns: by a grammatical convention *I, we, me, mine, us, ours* are called first person pronouns, since *they* refer to the speaker; *you* and *yours* are called second person pronouns, since *they* refer to the person addressed; and *he, him, his, she, hers, they, them, theirs* are called third person pronouns since *they* refer to the things or persons discussed. (2) Demonstrative pronouns: *this, that, these, those.* (3) Interrogative, or question, pronouns: *who, whom, what, whose, which.* (4) Relative pronouns, or pronouns *which* refer back to something already mentioned: *who, whom, that, which.* (5) Others: *some, any, anyone, no one, other, whichever, none,* etc.

Pronouns are difficult for *us*, since our categories are not as clear as in some other languages, and *we* use the same words for *what* foreign-language speakers see as different situations. First, our interrogative and relative pronouns overlap, and must be separated in translation. The easiest way is to observe whether a question is involved in the sentence. Examples: "*Which* [int.] do *you* like?" "The inn, *which* [rel.] was not far from Coimbra, had a restaurant." "*Who* [int.] is there?" "*I* don't know *who* [int.] was there." "The porter *who* [rel.] took our bags was Number 2132." *This* may seem to be a trivial difference to an English speaker, but in some languages *it* is very important.

Secondly, there is an overlap between pronouns and adjectives. In some cases the word "this," for example, is a pronoun; in other cases *it* is an adjective. *This* also holds true for *his, its, her, any, none, other, some, that, these, those,* and many other words. Note whether the word in question stands alone or is associated with another word. Examples: "*This* [pronoun] is *mine.*" "This [adj.] taxi has no springs." Watch out for the word "that," which can be a pronoun or an adjective or a conjunction. And remember that "my," "your," "our," and "their" are always adjectives. [All pronouns in this section are in italics.]

Prepositions. Prepositions are the little words that introduce phrases that tell *about* condition, time, place, manner, association, degree, and similar topics. Such words as *with, in, beside, under, of, to, about, for,* and *upon* are prepositions. In English prepositions and adverbs overlap, but, as you will see *by* checking *in* your dictionary, there are usually differences *of* meaning *between* the two uses. [Prepositions *in* this paragraph are designated *by* italics.]

Conjunctions. Conjunctions are joining-words. They enable you to link words *or* groups of words into larger units, *and* to build compound *or* complex sentences out of simple sentence units. Such words as *and, but, although, or, unless,* are typical conjunctions. *Although* most conjunctions are easy enough to identify, the word "that" should be watched closely to see *that* it is not a pronoun *or* an adjective. [Conjunctions italicized.]

Words about Verbs

Verbs are responsible for most of the terminology in this short grammar. The basic terms are:

Conjugation. In many languages verbs fall into natural groups, according to the way they make their forms. These groupings are called conjugations, and are an aid to learning grammatical structure. Though it may seem difficult at first to speak of First and Second Conjugations, these are simply short ways of saying that verbs belonging to these classes make their forms according to certain consistent rules, which you can memorize.

Infinitive. This is the basic form which most dictionaries give for verbs in most languages, and in most languages it serves as the basis for classifying verbs. In English (with a very few exceptions) it has no special form. To find the infinitive for any English verb, just fill in this sentence: "I like to .... (walk, run, jump, swim, carry, disappear, etc.)." The infinitive in English is usually preceded by the word "to."

Tense. This is simply a formal way of saying "time." In English we think of time as being broken into three great segments: past, present, and future. Our verbs are assigned forms to indicate this division, and are further subdivided for shades of meaning. We subdivide the present time into the present (I walk) and present progressive (I am walking); the past into the simple past (I walked), progressive past (I was walking), perfect or present perfect (I have walked), past perfect or pluperfect (I had walked); and future into simple future (I shall walk) and future progressive (I shall be walking.) These are the most common English tenses.

Present Participles, Progressive Tenses. In English the present participle always ends in *-ing.* It can be used as a noun or an adjective in some situations, but its chief use is in *forming* the so-called progressive tenses. These are made by *putting* appropriate forms of the verb "to be" before a present participle: For "to walk" [an infinitive], for example, the present progressive would be: I am *walking*, you are *walking*, he is *walking*, etc.; past progressive, I was *walking*, you were *walking*, and so on. [Present participles are in italics.]

Past Participles, Perfect Tenses.   The past participle in English is not *formed* as regularly as is the present participle.   Sometimes it is *constructed* by adding -ed or -d to the present tense, as *walked*, *jumped*, *looked*, *received*; but there are many verbs where it is *formed* less regularly: *seen, been, swum, chosen, brought*.   To find it, simply fill out the sentence "I have..........." putting in the verb form that your ear tells you is right for the particular verb.   If you speak grammatically, you will have the past participle.

Past participles are sometimes used as adjectives: "Don't cry over *spilt* milk."   Their most important use, however, is to form the system of verb tenses that are *called* the perfect tenses: present perfect (or perfect), past perfect (or pluperfect), etc.   In English the present perfect tense is *formed* with the present tense of "to have" and the past participle of a verb: I have *walked*, you have *run*, he has *begun*, etc.   The past perfect is *formed*, similarly, with the past tense of "to have" and the past participle: I had *walked*, you had *run*, he had *begun*.   Most of the languages you are likely to study have similar systems of perfect tenses, though they may not be *formed* in exactly the same way as in English.   [Past participles in italics.]

Preterit, Imperfect.   Many languages have more than one verb tense for expressing an action that took place in the past.   They may use a perfect tense (which we have just covered), or a preterit, or an imperfect.   English, although you may never have thought about it, is one of these languages, for we can say "I have spoken to him" [present perfect], or "I spoke to him" [simple past], or "I was speaking to him" [past progressive].   These sentences do not mean exactly the same thing, although the differences are subtle, and are difficult to put into other words.

While usage differs a little from language to language, if a language has both a preterit and an imperfect, in general the preterit corresponds to the English simple past (I ran, I swam, I spoke), and the imperfect corresponds to the English past progressive (I was running, I was swimming, I was speaking). If you are curious to discover the mode of thought behind these different tenses, try looking at the situation in terms of background-action and point-action. One of the most important uses of the imperfect is to provide a background against which a single point-action can take place. For example, "When I was walking down the street [background, continued over a period of time, hence past progressive or imperfect], I stubbed my toe [an instant or point of time, hence a simple past or preterit]."

Auxiliary Verbs.   Auxiliary verbs are special words that are used to help other verbs make their forms. In English, for example, we use forms of the verb "to have" in our perfect tenses: I have seen, you had come, he has been, etc. We also use *shall* or *will* to make our future tenses: I shall pay, you will see, etc. French, German, Spanish, Italian, and Portuguese also make use of auxiliary verbs, but although the same general concept is present, the use of auxiliaries differs very much from one language to another, and you must learn the practice for each language.

Reflexive.   This term, which sounds more difficult than it really is, simply means that the verb flexes back upon the noun or pronoun that is its subject. In modern English the reflexive pronoun always has -*self* on its end, and we do not use the construction very frequently. In other languages, however, reflexive forms may be used more frequently, and in ways that do not seem very logical to an English speaker. Examples of English reflexive sentences: "He washes himself." "He seated himself at the table."

Passive.   In some languages, like Latin, there is a strong feeling that an action or thing that is taking place can be expressed in two different ways. One can say, A does-something-to B, which is "active"; or B is-having-something-done-to-him by A, which is "passive." We do not have a strong feeling for this classification of experience in English, but the following examples should indicate the difference between an active and a passive verb: Active: "John is building a house." Passive: "A house is being built by John." Active: "The steamer carried the cotton to England." Passive: "The cotton was carried by the steamer to England." Bear in mind that the formation of passive verbs and the situations where they can be used vary enormously from language to language. This is one situation where you usually cannot translate English word for word into another language and make sense.

Impersonal Verbs. In English there are some verbs which do not have an ordinary subject, and do not refer to persons. They are always used with the pronoun *it*, which does not refer to anything specifically, but simply serves to fill out the verb forms. Examples: It is snowing. It hailed last night. It seems to me that you are wrong. It has been raining. It won't do.

Other languages, like German, have this same general concept, but impersonal verbs may differ quite a bit in form and frequency from one language to another.

Words about Nouns

Agreement. In some languages, where nouns or adjectives or articles are declined, or have gender endings, it is necessary that the adjective or article be in the same case or gender or number as the noun it goes with (modifies). This is called agreement.

This may be illustrated from Portuguese, where articles and adjectives have to agree with nouns in gender and number.

uma casa	one white	duas casas	two white
branca	house	brancas	houses
um cavalo	one white	dois cavalos	two white
branco	horse	brancos	horses

Here *uma* is feminine singular and has the ending -*a* because it agrees with the feminine singular noun *casa*; *branca* has the ending -*a* because it agrees with the feminine singular noun *casa*. *Branco*, on the other hand, and *um*, are masculine singular because *cavalo* is masculine singular.

Gender. Gender should not be confused with actual sex. In many languages nouns are arbitrarily assigned a gender (masculine or feminine, or masculine or feminine or neuter), and this need not correspond to sex. You simply have to learn the pattern of the language you are studying in order to become familiar with its use of gender.

Miscellaneous Terms

Comparative, Superlative. These two terms are used with adjectives and adverbs. They indicate the degree of strength within the meaning of the word. *Faster, better, earlier, newer, more rapid, more detailed, more suitable* are examples of the comparative in adjectives, while *more rapidly, more recently, more suitably* are comparatives for adverbs. In most cases, as you have seen, the comparative uses *-er* or "more" for an adjective, and "more" for an adverb. Superlatives are those forms which end in *-est* or have "most" placed before them for adjectives, and "most" prefixed for adverbs: *most intelligent, earliest, most rapidly, most suitably.*

Idiom. An idiom is an expression that is peculiar to a language, the meaning of which is not the same as the literal meaning of the individual words composing it. Idioms, as a rule, cannot be translated word by word into another language. Examples of English idioms: "*Take it easy.*" "Don't *beat around the bush.*" "It *turned out* to be *a Dutch treat.*" "Can you *tell time* in Portuguese?"

The Parts of the Sentence

Subject, Predicate. In grammar *every complete sentence* contains two basic parts, the subject and the predicate. *The subject, if we* state the terms most simply, is the thing, person, or activity talked about. *It* can be a noun, a pronoun, or something *that* serves as a noun. *A subject* would include, in a typical case, a noun, the articles or adjectives *which* are associated with it, and perhaps phrases. Note that, in complex sentences, *each part* may have its own subject. [*The subjects of the sentences above* have been italicized.]

The predicate *talks about the subject.* In a formal sentence the predicate *includes a verb, its adverbs, predicate adjectives, phrases, and objects*—whatever *happens to be present.* A predicate adjective *is an adjective* which *happens to be in the predicate after a form of the verb* "*to be.*" Example: "*Apples are red.*" [Predicates *are in italics.*]

In the following simple sentences subjects are in italics, predicates in italics and underlined. "*Green apples are bad for your digestion.*" "When *I go to Brazil, I always stop in São Paulo.*" "*The man with the handbag is travelling to Lisbon.*"

Direct and Indirect Objects. Some verbs (called transitive verbs) take direct and/or indirect objects in their predicates; other verbs (called intransitive verbs) do not take objects of any sort. In English, except for pronouns, objects do not have any special forms, but in languages which have case forms or more pronoun forms than English, objects can be troublesome.

The direct object is the person, thing, quality, or matter that the verb directs *its action* upon. It can be a pronoun, or a noun, perhaps accompanied by an article and/or adjectives. The direct object always directly follows *its verb*, except when there is also an indirect object pronoun present, which comes between the verb and the direct object. Prepositions do not go before direct objects. Examples: "The cook threw *green onions* into the stew." "The border guards will want to see *your passport* tomorrow." "Give *it* to me." "Please give me *a glass of red wine.*" [We have placed *direct objects* in this paragraph in italics.]

The indirect object, as grammars will tell *you*, is the person or thing for or to whom the action is taking place. It can be a pronoun or a noun with or without article and adjectives. In most cases the words "to" or "for" can be inserted before it, if not already there. Examples: "Please tell *me* the time." "I wrote *her* a letter from Bahia." "We sent *Mr. Fernandes* fifty escudos." "We gave *the most energetic guide* a large tip." [Indirect objects are in italics.]

INDEX

The following abbreviations have been used in this index: *adj.* for adjective, *def.* for definition, and *pron.* for pronoun. Portuguese words appear in *italic* and their English equivalents in parentheses.

A CATALOG OF SELECTED
DOVER BOOKS
IN ALL FIELDS OF INTEREST

A CATALOG OF SELECTED DOVER
BOOKS IN ALL FIELDS OF INTEREST

CONCERNING THE SPIRITUAL IN ART, Wassily Kandinsky. Pioneering work by father of abstract art. Thoughts on color theory, nature of art. Analysis of earlier masters. 12 illustrations. 80pp. of text. 5⅜ x 8½. 0-486-23411-8

CELTIC ART: The Methods of Construction, George Bain. Simple geometric techniques for making Celtic interlacements, spirals, Kells-type initials, animals, humans, etc. Over 500 illustrations. 160pp. 9 x 12. (Available in U.S. only.) 0-486-22923-8

AN ATLAS OF ANATOMY FOR ARTISTS, Fritz Schider. Most thorough reference work on art anatomy in the world. Hundreds of illustrations, including selections from works by Vesalius, Leonardo, Goya, Ingres, Michelangelo, others. 593 illustrations. 192pp. 7⅛ x 10¼. 0-486-20241-0

CELTIC HAND STROKE-BY-STROKE (Irish Half-Uncial from "The Book of Kells"): An Arthur Baker Calligraphy Manual, Arthur Baker. Complete guide to creating each letter of the alphabet in distinctive Celtic manner. Covers hand position, strokes, pens, inks, paper, more. Illustrated. 48pp. 8¼ x 11. 0-486-24336-2

EASY ORIGAMI, John Montroll. Charming collection of 32 projects (hat, cup, pelican, piano, swan, many more) specially designed for the novice origami hobbyist. Clearly illustrated easy-to-follow instructions insure that even beginning papercrafters will achieve successful results. 48pp. 8¼ x 11. 0-486-27298-2

BLOOMINGDALE'S ILLUSTRATED 1886 CATALOG: Fashions, Dry Goods and Housewares, Bloomingdale Brothers. Famed merchants' extremely rare catalog depicting about 1,700 products: clothing, housewares, firearms, dry goods, jewelry, more. Invaluable for dating, identifying vintage items. Also, copyright-free graphics for artists, designers. Co-published with Henry Ford Museum & Greenfield Village. 160pp. 8¼ x 11. 0-486-25780-0

THE ART OF WORLDLY WISDOM, Baltasar Gracian. "Think with the few and speak with the many," "Friends are a second existence," and "Be able to forget" are among this 1637 volume's 300 pithy maxims. A perfect source of mental and spiritual refreshment, it can be opened at random and appreciated either in brief or at length. 128pp. 5⅜ x 8½. 0-486-44034-6

JOHNSON'S DICTIONARY: A Modern Selection, Samuel Johnson (E. L. McAdam and George Milne, eds.). This modern version reduces the original 1755 edition's 2,300 pages of definitions and literary examples to a more manageable length, retaining the verbal pleasure and historical curiosity of the original. 480pp. 5³⁄₁₆ x 8¼. 0-486-44089-3

ADVENTURES OF HUCKLEBERRY FINN, Mark Twain, Illustrated by E. W. Kemble. A work of eternal richness and complexity, a source of ongoing critical debate, and a literary landmark, Twain's 1885 masterpiece about a barefoot boy's journey of self-discovery has enthralled readers around the world. This handsome clothbound reproduction of the first edition features all 174 of the original black-and-white illustrations. 368pp. 5⅜ x 8½. 0-486-44322-1

STICKLEY CRAFTSMAN FURNITURE CATALOGS, Gustav Stickley and L. & J. G. Stickley. Beautiful, functional furniture in two authentic catalogs from 1910. 594 illustrations, including 277 photos, show settles, rockers, armchairs, reclining chairs, bookcases, desks, tables. 183pp. 6½ x 9¼. 0-486-23838-5

AMERICAN LOCOMOTIVES IN HISTORIC PHOTOGRAPHS: 1858 to 1949, Ron Ziel (ed.). A rare collection of 126 meticulously detailed official photographs, called "builder portraits," of American locomotives that majestically chronicle the rise of steam locomotive power in America. Introduction. Detailed captions. xi+ 129pp. 9 x 12. 0-486-27393-8

AMERICA'S LIGHTHOUSES: An Illustrated History, Francis Ross Holland, Jr. Delightfully written, profusely illustrated fact-filled survey of over 200 American lighthouses since 1716. History, anecdotes, technological advances, more. 240pp. 8 x 10¾. 0-486-25576-X

TOWARDS A NEW ARCHITECTURE, Le Corbusier. Pioneering manifesto by founder of "International School." Technical and aesthetic theories, views of industry, economics, relation of form to function, "mass-production split" and much more. Profusely illustrated. 320pp. 6⅛ x 9¼. (Available in U.S. only.) 0-486-25023-7

HOW THE OTHER HALF LIVES, Jacob Riis. Famous journalistic record, exposing poverty and degradation of New York slums around 1900, by major social reformer. 100 striking and influential photographs. 233pp. 10 x 7⅛. 0-486-22012-5

FRUIT KEY AND TWIG KEY TO TREES AND SHRUBS, William M. Harlow. One of the handiest and most widely used identification aids. Fruit key covers 120 deciduous and evergreen species; twig key 160 deciduous species. Easily used. Over 300 photographs. 126pp. 5⅜ x 8½. 0-486-20511-8

COMMON BIRD SONGS, Dr. Donald J. Borror. Songs of 60 most common U.S. birds: robins, sparrows, cardinals, bluejays, finches, more–arranged in order of increasing complexity. Up to 9 variations of songs of each species.
Cassette and manual 0-486-99911-4

ORCHIDS AS HOUSE PLANTS, Rebecca Tyson Northen. Grow cattleyas and many other kinds of orchids–in a window, in a case, or under artificial light. 63 illustrations. 148pp. 5⅜ x 8½. 0-486-23261-1

MONSTER MAZES, Dave Phillips. Masterful mazes at four levels of difficulty. Avoid deadly perils and evil creatures to find magical treasures. Solutions for all 32 exciting illustrated puzzles. 48pp. 8¼ x 11. 0-486-26005-4

MOZART'S DON GIOVANNI (DOVER OPERA LIBRETTO SERIES), Wolfgang Amadeus Mozart. Introduced and translated by Ellen H. Bleiler. Standard Italian libretto, with complete English translation. Convenient and thoroughly portable–an ideal companion for reading along with a recording or the performance itself. Introduction. List of characters. Plot summary. 121pp. 5¼ x 8½. 0-486-24944-1

FRANK LLOYD WRIGHT'S DANA HOUSE, Donald Hoffmann. Pictorial essay of residential masterpiece with over 160 interior and exterior photos, plans, elevations, sketches and studies. 128pp. 9¼ x 10¾. 0-486-29120-0

A MODERN HERBAL, Margaret Grieve. Much the fullest, most exact, most useful compilation of herbal material. Gigantic alphabetical encyclopedia, from aconite to zedoary, gives botanical information, medical properties, folklore, economic uses, much else. Indispensable to serious reader. 161 illustrations. 888pp. 6½ x 9¼. 2-vol. set. (Available in U.S. only.)   Vol. I: 0-486-22798-7   Vol. II: 0-486-22799-5

HIDDEN TREASURE MAZE BOOK, Dave Phillips. Solve 34 challenging mazes accompanied by heroic tales of adventure. Evil dragons, people-eating plants, blood-thirsty giants, many more dangerous adversaries lurk at every twist and turn. 34 mazes, stories, solutions. 48pp. 8¼ x 11.   0-486-24566-7

LETTERS OF W. A. MOZART, Wolfgang A. Mozart. Remarkable letters show bawdy wit, humor, imagination, musical insights, contemporary musical world; includes some letters from Leopold Mozart. 276pp. 5⅜ x 8½.   0-486-22859-2

BASIC PRINCIPLES OF CLASSICAL BALLET, Agrippina Vaganova. Great Russian theoretician, teacher explains methods for teaching classical ballet. 118 illustrations. 175pp. 5⅜ x 8½.   0-486-22036-2

THE JUMPING FROG, Mark Twain. Revenge edition. The original story of The Celebrated Jumping Frog of Calaveras County, a hapless French translation, and Twain's hilarious "retranslation" from the French. 12 illustrations. 66pp. 5⅜ x 8½.
0-486-22686-7

BEST REMEMBERED POEMS, Martin Gardner (ed.). The 126 poems in this superb collection of 19th- and 20th-century British and American verse range from Shelley's "To a Skylark" to the impassioned "Renascence" of Edna St. Vincent Millay and to Edward Lear's whimsical "The Owl and the Pussycat." 224pp. 5⅜ x 8½.
0-486-27165-X

COMPLETE SONNETS, William Shakespeare. Over 150 exquisite poems deal with love, friendship, the tyranny of time, beauty's evanescence, death and other themes in language of remarkable power, precision and beauty. Glossary of archaic terms. 80pp. 5³⁄₁₆ x 8¼.   0-486-26686-9

HISTORIC HOMES OF THE AMERICAN PRESIDENTS, Second, Revised Edition, Irvin Haas. A traveler's guide to American Presidential homes, most open to the public, depicting and describing homes occupied by every American President from George Washington to George Bush. With visiting hours, admission charges, travel routes. 175 photographs. Index. 160pp. 8¼ x 11.   0-486-26751-2

THE WIT AND HUMOR OF OSCAR WILDE, Alvin Redman (ed.). More than 1,000 ripostes, paradoxes, wisecracks: Work is the curse of the drinking classes; I can resist everything except temptation; etc. 258pp. 5⅜ x 8½.   0-486-20602-5

SHAKESPEARE LEXICON AND QUOTATION DICTIONARY, Alexander Schmidt. Full definitions, locations, shades of meaning in every word in plays and poems. More than 50,000 exact quotations. 1,485pp. 6½ x 9¼. 2-vol. set.
Vol. 1: 0-486-22726-X   Vol. 2: 0-486-22727-8

SELECTED POEMS, Emily Dickinson. Over 100 best-known, best-loved poems by one of America's foremost poets, reprinted from authoritative early editions. No comparable edition at this price. Index of first lines. 64pp. 5³⁄₁₆ x 8¼. 0-486-26466-1

THE INSIDIOUS DR. FU-MANCHU, Sax Rohmer. The first of the popular mystery series introduces a pair of English detectives to their archnemesis, the diabolical Dr. Fu-Manchu. Flavorful atmosphere, fast-paced action, and colorful characters enliven this classic of the genre. 208pp. 5³⁄₁₆ x 8¼.   0-486-29898-1

LIGHT AND SHADE: A Classic Approach to Three-Dimensional Drawing, Mrs. Mary P. Merrifield. Handy reference clearly demonstrates principles of light and shade by revealing effects of common daylight, sunshine, and candle or artificial light on geometrical solids. 13 plates. 64pp. 5⅜ x 8½. 0-486-44143-1

ASTROLOGY AND ASTRONOMY: A Pictorial Archive of Signs and Symbols, Ernst and Johanna Lehner. Treasure trove of stories, lore, and myth, accompanied by more than 300 rare illustrations of planets, the Milky Way, signs of the zodiac, comets, meteors, and other astronomical phenomena. 192pp. 8⅜ x 11.

0-486-43981-X

JEWELRY MAKING: Techniques for Metal, Tim McCreight. Easy-to-follow instructions and carefully executed illustrations describe tools and techniques, use of gems and enamels, wire inlay, casting, and other topics. 72 line illustrations and diagrams. 176pp. 8¼ x 10⅞. 0-486-44043-5

MAKING BIRDHOUSES: Easy and Advanced Projects, Gladstone Califf. Easy-to-follow instructions include diagrams for everything from a one-room house for bluebirds to a forty-two-room structure for purple martins. 56 plates; 4 figures. 80pp. 8¾ x 6⅜. 0-486-44183-0

LITTLE BOOK OF LOG CABINS: How to Build and Furnish Them, William S. Wicks. Handy how-to manual, with instructions and illustrations for building cabins in the Adirondack style, fireplaces, stairways, furniture, beamed ceilings, and more. 102 line drawings. 96pp. 8¾ x 6⅜. 0-486-44259-4

THE SEASONS OF AMERICA PAST, Eric Sloane. From "sugaring time" and strawberry picking to Indian summer and fall harvest, a whole year's activities described in charming prose and enhanced with 79 of the author's own illustrations. 160pp. 8¼ x 11. 0-486-44220-9

THE METROPOLIS OF TOMORROW, Hugh Ferriss. Generous, prophetic vision of the metropolis of the future, as perceived in 1929. Powerful illustrations of towering structures, wide avenues, and rooftop parks—all features in many of today's modern cities. 59 illustrations. 144pp. 8¼ x 11. 0-486-43727-2

THE PATH TO ROME, Hilaire Belloc. This 1902 memoir abounds in lively vignettes from a vanished time, recounting a pilgrimage on foot across the Alps and Apennines in order to "see all Europe which the Christian Faith has saved." 77 of the author's original line drawings complement his sparkling prose. 272pp. 5⅜ x 8½.

0-486-44001-X

THE HISTORY OF RASSELAS: Prince of Abissinia, Samuel Johnson. Distinguished English writer attacks eighteenth-century optimism and man's unrealistic estimates of what life has to offer. 112pp. 5⅜ x 8½. 0-486-44094-X

A VOYAGE TO ARCTURUS, David Lindsay. A brilliant flight of pure fancy, where wild creatures crowd the fantastic landscape and demented torturers dominate victims with their bizarre mental powers. 272pp. 5⅜ x 8½. 0-486-44198-9

Paperbound unless otherwise indicated. Available at your book dealer, online at **www.doverpublications.com**, or by writing to Dept. GI, Dover Publications, Inc., 31 East 2nd Street, Mineola, NY 11501. For current price information or for free catalogs (please indicate field of interest), write to Dover Publications or log on to **www.doverpublications.com** and see every Dover book in print. Dover publishes more than 400 books each year on science, elementary and advanced mathematics, biology, music, art, literary history, social sciences, and other areas.